Jerome Markowitz built his first experimental organ in 1936, and, with the exception of the World War II years, continued his work until his death on February 13, 1991. This second printing of *Triumphs and Trials of an Organ Builder* is a tribute to a remarkable individual who has touched the lives of countless people throughout the world.

Triumphs & Trials
of an Organ Builder

Jerome Markowitz

First Edition, Second Printing
987654321

TRIUMPHS AND TRIALS OF AN ORGAN BUILDER

Copyright ©   1989 by Jerome Markowitz.

ISBN 0-9624896-0-3

Printed in the United States of America

Contents

Acknowledgments

Obviously, neither this book nor the very existence of Allen Organ Company would have been possible without the support of our many customers and ardent enthusiasts—the people who have been intimately involved in the recommendation, specification and purchase of the more than 50,000 Allen Organs. As I look back over fifty years in the organ business, I am faced with a seemingly endless list of people who have given their warm support.

I firmly believe that there is a unique relationship between Allen Organ Company and each purchaser of an Allen Organ—and a unique story to be told in each case. However, given this overwhelmingly long list of people to thank, I can't even begin to individually acknowledge them in this small space. Accordingly, I sincerely hope that they will accept my apology for not mentioning each and every one of them by name.

And certainly, to our dedicated employees, both current and retired, goes my heartfelt thanks. These are the people who skillfully handle the myriad details from the construction of the organ to its ultimate sale.

Then there is our dealer organization, including both entrepreneurs and sales personnel who have steadfastly supported us—many for decades. Their efforts are most gratefully acknowledged.

I must recognize those wonderful virtuoso organists and recitalists whose support is so greatly appreciated. Again, having such a long list of people to individually thank, I hope they will accept my collective "thank you."

Additionally, I would like to acknowledge that the writing of this book could hardly have been possible without the invaluable assistance and collaboration of Robert Woron. Also, a special thanks to my secretary, Carolyn Lahr, who used her total command of word processors and the gift of endless patience to efficiently type and retype the numerous drafts of the manuscript as the book gradually came together.

Finally, thanks to my wife, Martha, for her critical reading of the manuscript as it evolved, her always perceptive comments, and her unwavering encouragement.

JEROME MARKOWITZ
Allentown, Pennsylvania

Preface

There are several reasons for my writing this book.

First, I want to completely answer those who have often asked me, "How on earth did you get into the organ business?

Second, there is so much "fabricated or improvised" history now being spread throughout the organ industry that there is a desperate need for some sober truth. Although I admit to having been reticent in the past—some might even say monastically discreet—I now want to speak out loudly and clearly. Because I have been blessed with 50 years of influencing the "recent" history of organ building, I have much to say about the organ industry based on firsthand knowledge. Indeed, if I could say everything I wanted to say, it would fill several books. Yet, I don't want to meander. Therefore, I have made every effort to speak effectively in order to provide the reader with useful, meticulously-researched, accurate information about some recent history of the organ industry from my unique vantage point.

Third, my years as an American businessman exposed me to problems typical of the problems being faced by other businessmen today. I feel that sharing my experience in dealing with these problems may help those facing similar problems.

And lastly, for the broader audience, I believe the book may also appeal to those who simply want to extend their knowledge into the mysterious world of organ building. However, don't expect to find long, detailed, highly-technical dissertations about how organs work. That is not the purpose of the book. The book is aimed mainly at the human interest side of the story; I hope it will be easily read, easily understood, as well as entertaining.

The beginning chapters of the book are organized chronologically while later chapters are more topical. The chapters may be thought of as a collection of essays each one substantially independent of the others in subject matter and style. Although it would be best to read the chapters sequentially, feel free to jump around.

I have made every effort to distinguish between what is fact and what is my opinion. It is important to me that you, the reader, know that when I portray something as fact in this book, it is based on solid supportive evidence. When I make an assertion based on my own perceptions, I will indicate it as such, and, no matter how strongly I believe in the truth of my assertions, I would suggest that you draw your own conclusions.

This book is about the organ industry in general and Allen Organ Company in particular. The industry's total, worldwide sales at the producer's level are less than $200 million a year. Picture a company in this industry with facilities for producing not only fine woodwork but also high-tech electronic systems—a company whose products are musical instruments. This is Allen Organ Company—the company whose organ sounded the first note played before an audience at the opening of Philharmonic Hall, Lincoln Center in 1962.

Allen's products are found in 50,000 churches in the U.S.A. and around the world. The Allen Organ has been called "fantastic" by Seiji Ozawa and referred to as "magnifique" by Herbert von Karajan. However, the implicit endorsement of Allen's products by satisfied customers has been bitterly attacked by a relatively small group of pipe organ "purists" who not only perceive each Allen installation as a personal threat (for reasons that are not quite clear) but also have used various means, both fair and foul, to try to stifle Allen's sales.

Imagine an industry whose products are only vaguely understood by most people who purchase them—people who often depend on local "experts" to "guide" them in making the most critical decisions. Picture a band of these "experts," some tightly organized into a closed society seemingly bulwarked against progress in the art of building the very product about which they profess their expertise.

Picture an industry with a most savage, competitive ambience and a Company forced into continuous litigations in attempts to protect its turf. Dear reader, enter the arcane world of organs. Jerome Markowitz, President of Allen Organ Company, will guide you.

Triumphs & Trials
of an Organ Builder

And there's another lesson I learned early on for which I'm very grateful. Getting so involved with the nitty-gritty of those early projects gave me a certain intimacy with the real, physical world—street wisdom, in a sense. I tapped this wisdom many times over the years. As President of Allen Organ Company, the world's largest producer of institutional electronic organs, I've had to size up many situations—from the very positive to the disturbingly negative, from applauding the "right stuff" to dealing with shameless frauds.

Who
Charts
the Course

As a youngster, I never planned to start my own company and "live happily ever after" as my own boss. However, there was obviously enough of a free-spirited nature born and bred into me to pull me in that direction.

My father had his own business. Not surprisingly, his plan for me was that I would get a standard education and then become part of his company. His plan failed. It was nobody's fault, really. I tried to honor his advice, but my heart wasn't in it. The "spirit" kept moving me in other directions.

In my early youth, of course, I lived with my parents and went to school like everyone else. This was in Jamaica, Long Island, New York, around 1930. My constant preoccupation with do-it-yourself projects confounded my efforts at school; my parents wanted me to spend more time on my school work. I can only imagine their distress as they contemplated their son's future. I know they were irritated with me at this point.

For the most part, my early "extracurricular" activity with gadgetry was met by family and friends with only mild interest at best. However, I think one of my projects at that time did, in fact, cause a bit of a stir. I built a television set. Television was, for most people, more in the realm of science fiction than reality. However, I knew about the experimental television transmissions being made at that time from radio station W2XBS in New York City. They had gone on the air with so-called "radiovision," using mechanical scanning equipment in 1928. I rigged up a receiving apparatus and managed to get a picture. It was crude by today's standards, but I believe I can safely boast that we were the first on our block to have a TV.

My parents, wanting the best for me, decided to send me away to Allentown Prep School. My father's factory was located in Allentown, Pennsylvania; conveniently, my sister lived there with her husband who worked for my father at the factory. I stayed at her home while I went through the Prep School and then on to Muhlenberg College. I believe my parents hoped that sending me to Allentown would get me to settle down into a more traditional path and devote my time to schooling. Well, I settled down in Allentown all right, but the forces at play inside me constantly put me at odds with my parents' desire for me to get a standard education. I kept delving into radio (which eventually led me into the world of organs and the generation of musical tones). I was captivated by what was then an obscure field. I didn't know at the time that radio would soon blossom into the fabulous world of electronics, and that I would be playing a role in it.

As for my academic education, I kept it up for a few years but without great enthusiasm. Then one day in February, 1937, I was struck down with appendix-related peritonitis. In those days, as I believe it is even today, peritonitis is very serious indeed. I was at death's door, a subject I paid little attention to before that time. Fortunately, I was able to walk out of the hospital a month later back on the road to health but a lot "older." A few months later, I left college. I would forever more chart my own course.

The Birth of the Electronic Organ

During the early 1930s, my radio projects taught me much about the emerging field of electronics. This put me into a knowledgeable position regarding electronic oscillators. As events in my life unfolded, this knowledge of oscillators was ultimately put to use in the development of the first commercially successful electronic organ.

As a youngster, I grew up hearing pipe organs in movie theaters and on the radio; I had always liked their sound. Later on, while attending Muhlenberg College in Allentown, I enjoyed the mandatory chapel on Thursday mornings when Dr. Marks, the Chairman of the Music Department, played the organ. The intricate patterns of sound created by the big, sustained chords especially fascinated me. Of course, in those early days, I didn't have the facility to fully understand what

I was hearing. Deeper insight into sound structures in terms of their spectral components would come later.

Interestingly, the pursuit of an amateur radio operator's license indirectly introduced me to my first tone generator. Getting the license required learning the Morse code. I learned the code, as most people did, by practicing on a device consisting of a key-switch connected to a simple tone generator. As I tapped out the code pattern on the key, the tone generator would beep back at me, faithfully generating an on/off pattern in synchronism with whatever patterns I chose to "key in." That's when the idea hit me. If I built a group of oscillators similar to those I built for my radio equipment but tuned to the various musical frequencies, I could connect these oscillators to the keys of an organ keyboard—the whole thing flashed through my mind. I could build an organ using electronic oscillators!

Some quick experiments with hardware convinced me that I was on to something, and I decided to find out more about organs and previous attempts at building "non-pipe" organs—organ-like instruments.

I found out that there were two electromechanical, organ-like instruments in existence at the time. One was an experimental device I'd heard on the radio which was constructed and played by a former military man, Captain Ranger. He referred to the instrument he played as the "Rangertone." I found out that its method of tone generation was based on a complex arrangement of rotating, electromechanical disks. The other was the

Hammond Organ, which was just beginning to appear on the market and rapidly gaining a following, especially in the field of popular music. It was also based on a variation of the rotating disk concept. At that time, finding and hearing a Hammond presented a bit of a challenge because only three or four such organs existed in all of New York City in 1936. However, I finally located one in a tavern in Queens. In my judgment, the instrument had a very ear-tickling sound, but my ears were also telling me that the sound it made was quite different from the sound of a pipe organ.

I continued to work on my own oscillator-based idea not knowing exactly where it would end; my first attempts were most crude. Eventually my apparatus functioned well enough for me to risk the scrutiny of some local organists. Luckily, their remarks were quite encouraging. They told me that my instrument "suggested" the sound of a pipe organ.

I remember, around that same time, talking to a boyhood friend, Bill Lenahan, who had become a church organist. He took me to his church where I had my first chance to hear a pipe organ at close range. Clearly, my rudimentary instrument sounded more like that pipe organ than a Hammond. I pressed on encouraged.

My immediate goal became clear. I was going to design and build a practical, electronic organ based on vacuum tube oscillators which would closely emulate the magnificent sound of the pipe organ. I was driven mainly by my technical curiosity; however, admittedly, fantasies of someday marketing an electronic organ began fluttering through my mind at this point. I learned that this idea had been approached by others but never marketed because of various technical flaws.

As I persevered, the main problem I encountered with the oscillator-based organ was tuning drift. Pipe organs have a similar problem, but my early oscillator designs were so drift prone that the instrument would not stay in tune long enough to be practical. Finally, after considerable effort, I discovered the solution to the tuning problem—a major breakthrough. I applied for a patent on my "stable oscillator" on October 27, 1937. The patent was granted on December 13, 1938. The brand-new, electronic organ technology was in my hands. I now was faced with what to do with it.

Getting to First Base

I had managed to make contact with the ball, so to speak, by devising and patenting a stable oscillator, enabling me to build experimental models of the electronic organ. In actual ball playing, the base running occurs in a matter of seconds. However, in the game of business, running the bases can take months, even years. This is where I "was" back in the late 1930s in Allentown—trying to find and get to first base after my initial success.

After my parents moved to Allentown, in 1937, I took over their basement where I set up a workshop to work on my organ venture. I was filled with excitement and all kinds of ideas. Periodically, I made trips to the Masonic Temple in Allentown to rent time on their pipe organ. As I recall, they charged a rather modest fee. This service was set up in order for organists to be able to get their hands on an organ for practice. It was ideal for my purposes, also. I was able to learn much about how organs are supposed to work and how they are supposed to sound through this hands-on experience.

Because of the great complexity of most organs, my projects came to require more work than I could do by myself in a reasonable time. I was able to get help from George Ehrig, a fellow ham radio enthusiast from Allentown. At that time, getting help was relatively easy because the country was still in the grip of the Depression, and people were quite happy to help out for whatever I could afford to pay them.

Actually, the Depression influenced my progress in several ways. As I just mentioned, I needed assistance to capitalize on my ideas; luckily for me, good people were available. I also needed parts and materials. I knew that some of the items I needed were probably lying unused somewhere because of the economic conditions. With this in mind, I became rather adept at sniffing out sources of supply. For example, I remember obtaining an unfinished organ console from a pipe organ builder in New Jersey. He was happy to unload it for a few dollars; I was happy to latch on to it to keep the venture rolling.

On the electronics end, I needed large, air-core coils for the oscillators. Today, it could take months to fulfill an order for these special coils. There would have to be specifications written, quotations sought, purchase orders issued, lead times to consider, invoices to process, etc. However, back in the late 1930s, things were different. To get my coils, I drove to New York City to a shop where these large coils could be wound. The owners, two brothers, had few orders. Therefore, on the drive to New York I merely made some intelligent guesses as to the number of turns and, when I got to the shop, simply described what I wanted. They wound my coils as I waited and took what I was able to pay after which I left for Allentown with the coils in hand.

The Depression also had negative influences on my getting around the bases. In the early phases of this inventive effort, the idea of becoming a manufacturer of organs could not be seriously considered. I didn't have the resources to manufacture consoles, to obtain mechanical and electronic parts, or to obtain all the assembly required. I thought of myself primarily as an inventor experimenting in a basement workshop with a lot of surplus radio parts. In fact, an article about me appeared in the Allentown *Evening Chronicle* of July 10, 1939. One of the reporters for the newspaper was an amateur organist. He heard about my work through the organists' "grapevine" and thought it would produce an interesting article. I was glowingly referred to as a "22-year-old Alexander Graham Bell." This was all enormously gratifying to me. However, deep down I realized that such accolades would be short-lived; any lasting success in following through on my electronic organ idea had to rest on a firmer foundation in the commercial world, Depression or not.

Because of my lack of resources, I tried to get some established organ manufacturers interested in producing an organ based on my ideas. I remember visiting people from the following companies: M. P. Moeller, Aeolian Skinner, and Kilgen Organ Company. The reception I received was generally cool except for Kilgen, where representatives were initially enthusiastic. I even had fairly serious discussions with the President, Eugene Kilgen. Ultimately, nothing ever came out of them. Perhaps the long Depression had drained the spirit of

Experimental home-type instrument built in 1938 using a 1930's vintage radio cabinet with electronics played from a 39-note accordion keyboard.

adventure from these established companies. I also tried to get something going with several piano companies, but I soon realized that although pianos and organs are both keyboard instruments, their manufacturers are worlds apart. The piano people could not help me either. It became clear that I would have to continue driving this venture on my own.

Prior to producing a full-size organ, I built two abbreviated instruments—one with an accordion keyboard and a larger unit including forty-nine,

Experimental forty-nine note version—1939.

piano-type keys. I moved the larger unit to the Hotel New Yorker in New York City and invited various people from companies that were established in that area to view the instrument. However, nothing tangible resulted from these demonstrations.

At some point during this time frame, the possibility of using an empty section of my father's textile factory arose. Meanwhile, he had become accustomed to my "tinkering." Because the basement of our home was becoming crowded, I opted for the factory; this turned out to be a good move. The factory maintenance man, Norman Koons, proved to have innumerable mechanical skills. Together, we designed an organ console on paper; Norman was convinced he could

Console of "Allen Organ No. 1" built by Norman Koons—1939.

build the console. I knew that I needed to somehow assemble a serious organ—one that could be played like a pipe organ, one that would sound like a pipe organ, one that I might even sell! Well, I gave Norman the go-ahead to build the console, and he did an amazingly professional job. Allen Organ No. 1 was underway. His sixteen-year-old son, Norman Koons, Jr., joined the team as an after-school helper and proved to be quite adept at following the circuit diagrams and doing the wiring and other electronic construction tasks. Within six months, we had the first, complete, demonstration organ using electronic oscillators. I decided to call it the "Allen Organ" after Allentown.

In anticipation of completing the demo organ, I had prepared a brochure. So, as soon as the organ was finished, I put on my salesman's hat, prepared myself for some selling, and took to the street. One prospect was the St. Catharine of Siena Roman Catholic Church in Allentown. They had a "pump" organ, and I thought I might have a chance at convincing the Rev. Hugh McMullan to give up this old reed organ in favor of the revolutionary, new, electronic organ. My sales pitch must have struck the right chord because the pastor of St. Catharine of Siena bought that first Allen in early 1940. In retrospect, I am amazed that Rev. McMullan took a chance on replacing the venerable reed organ with a radically different, unproven piece of equipment. He might have viewed the instrument as just another newfangled contraption and summarily dismissed it.

Happily, he liked what he saw and heard; the organ was installed shortly thereafter. I am gratified to know that this first Allen reliably served that congregation for many years until 1953 when St. Catharine's moved to a newly built cathedral next door. Moreover, our relationship with this Church did not end there—but more on that later.

Shortly after the first Allen was installed at St. Catharine's, I received an expression of interest from Ray Trainer, the proprietor of Trainer's Restaurant in

Allen technician, James Wetherhold, viewing
a tone generator rack built in 1941.

Quakertown, Pennsylvania. Trainer's was a large and very popular place located a few miles south of Allentown. Part of their formula for success hinged on the broad appeal of their organ entertainment. They had an Everett Orgatron at the time. The Orgatron was an instrument, based on a vibrating reed principle, which sounded somewhat like a melodion. After some hard bargaining, a deal was struck; the second Allen organ went to Trainer's. The organist, Bill Andrews, seemed delighted.

By late 1941, I had taken a third order, from Temple Keneseth Israel in Allentown, for an electronic organ to replace a twenty-five-year-old pipe organ which had seen better days. But before the delivery of this instrument could be accomplished in early 1942, a cataclysmic event occurred. The news of it came to me over my car radio. The Japanese had bombed Pearl Harbor. A tiny country half way around the world had managed to shake the very foundations of our mighty nation, not to mention my fledgling operation. The Keneseth Israel organ would be completed, but it was quite clear that my electronic organ venture would have to be mothballed. By spring, 1942, World War II was upon us, and I became employed by the military as a civilian electronics engineer.

I had gotten to first base all right, but the game was postponed because of forces way beyond my control. Fortunately, the story does not end here. Our country survived; I survived. The project would resume.

The
Venture
Resumes

By early-to-mid 1945, the return of American industry to peaceful pursuits seemed apparent. I was eager to get back to being an electronic organ builder. Also, I was hoping that as the country returned to peace, I would be able to dust off the operation I had mothballed years earlier and get back in the game. After all, my efforts in the organ business up to that point had "only" gotten me to first base. I was determined to go farther.

There were plenty of problems back in '45. For openers, parts were very scarce and funds were low. Fortunately, the lessons and survival skills I learned in my "early" years were still intact.

I remember that somewhere in this time frame I got an inquiry from Harold Steinbright, an executive at a chemical company who was an organ enthusiast. He told me an amazing story. The former owner of the chemical company, Mr. Grevel, had also been an organ buff who had commissioned an electronic organ experimenter—someone I had vaguely known about—to build him an electronic organ. Before the organ could be made to function, Grevel died. Because he had no surviving family or close associates, Grevel left the entire company to the employees along with the incomplete organ and parts inventory. As I recall, some of this story was covered by newspapers at the time. The company's new owners terminated work on the organ and put it into storage. The experimenter, Spencer McKellip, later became a consultant for C. G. Conn's organ division, which produced electronic organs from approximately 1947 into the early 1980s when production ceased.

Mr. Steinbright decided that he, too, wanted an organ and called me for a proposal to be tied into the unfinished organ and parts. I suppose he heard about my earlier successes by word-of-mouth and concluded that I could provide what he wanted. I jumped at the chance. I sorely needed the parts from that unfinished organ and the associated inventory being stored at his factory. We struck a deal. He obtained an Allen organ; I received a goodly quantity of scarce parts. These parts eventually helped me get some more organs out into the field which, in turn, exposed me to still more organ enthusiasts. At this stage in the venture, getting this kind of exposure was of prime importance.

I was never too busy to talk to people about organs and the organ business. Luckily, others shared my interest in the subject. They heard classical organ music in their church and popular organ music from the Hammond on the radio, in movies, and at concerts. I truly enjoyed talking to people about all aspects of the organ field. However, I must admit that because of limited, personal funds I very often would find myself scrutinizing these good folks for any signs of their having some spare cash—money that "I" knew could be put to use as an investment in Allen Organ Company.

At some point during the first half of 1945, I decided that Allen Organ Company should become a corporation which subsequently occurred on July 17, 1945. I reasoned that a "corporate" structure would make a strong statement that the Allen Organ Company was "for real" and that I was committed to turning my hometown venture into a full-blown, business enterprise. It also allowed me to solicit investment money from friends and relatives in the traditional way—by selling stock. My initial effort was moderately successful; the Corporation obtained enough capital to lease factory space, to buy some equipment, and to hire some people. By the end of the year, the Company had fifteen employees, a cabinet shop for building consoles and pedalboards, an electronics area, and a small testing area.

In 1946, I was able to sell eight to ten organs all in the local area. This along with acquired capital was enough to keep the Company going. In fact, my confidence was high enough to allow me to move to a new location at 8th and Pittston Streets in Allentown, which provided 14,000 square feet of leased factory space. Also, in this time frame, I realized that I could not adequately handle sales, engineering, accounting, production, personnel, and supervision myself. So, I asked a college friend, Michale J. MyLymuk, about joining the Company as shop manager; he agreed. He played an important role in the day-to-day operation of the company and eventually became Vice President of Production. There was an element of fate in our relationship. We became friends because we sat near each other in various classes at Muhlenberg; also, we both had some common hobbies. We sat near each other in college only because seating students in alphabetical order was customary in those days.

I must say that the Allentown area seemed to be an ideal place to set up the Company back in 1946. There was a good supply of capable "radio technicians" and cabinetmakers who responded to my help-wanted ads. The people of the area were known for their conscientious hard work. In addition, I related well to them. Again, fate was on my side by placing me in the right place at that critical time in the life of the Company.

Building
a Viable
Company

From 1946 to the early 1950s, I fought hard for the survival of Allen Organ Company. Often, the money coming in from sales was not enough to cover expenses. At the end of 1946, I was forced to lay off a few employees. It was very troubling for me to have to let good people go. I imagined the distress they must have felt at suddenly being without a job; I felt a heavy burden of responsibility. I know that layoffs are commonly used by companies to solve cash flow problems, but this tactic was not at all palatable to me. In the years that followed, we struggled through cyclical, downward business conditions without resorting to layoffs. In retrospect, I believe Allen Organ Company has been aided in establishing itself as the leading manufacturer of institutional organs partly because of this no-layoff policy.

Some other important Allen Organ "philosophies" evolved during this time period. Most of the organs we built went into churches. I sensed early on that churches are bastions of permanence. For example, when I went into a church, I observed stained glass windows with the names of people long since departed but not forgotten. Outside, the world appeared to be rather unpredictable with its many issues, events, and interests that emerged daily but quickly receded from relevance. But inside these churches there was a distinct ambiance of predictability, stability, and lasting values. I wanted Allen organs to fit comfortably into this ambiance of permanence. Therefore, I wanted Allen organs to be built to last.

Our organs would carry multi-year guarantees and could be serviced indefinitely. This was an ambitious strategy, especially in the vacuum tube days. For example, in the months following the end of the War, we could only obtain military-surplus tubes. However, these tubes were surprisingly reliable. I remember that when commercial tube production was resumed after the War, we tried the new tubes but encountered some reliability problems. Through a very knowledgeable friend at the Western Electric plant in Allentown, I received some suggestions. As a result, we learned how to vastly enhance tube reliability through special circuit design techniques. Today, there are hundreds of Allen vacuum tube organs in operation and still serving satisfied customers well. This permanence-of-service policy paid off. We can now point with pride to many customers who have enjoyed our instruments for years, even decades, without fear of abandonment.

Another philosophy became firmly implanted during these formative years in the history of the Company. Top priority was given to the quality of the sound. There are many opportunities to cut corners in designing an organ. Often, the resulting deficiencies are not readily apparent to the listener. Many times— as I had discovered early on in my organ venture— even organists and good listeners may not immediately "pick up" these deficiencies. However, I believe that, after people live with an organ for a time, many of the listeners and certainly the organists will become aware of such deficiencies and the organ will gradually fall out of favor. This scenario is what I wanted to avoid. I knew that customers would be "living" with the Allen organs they bought for many years; to stay in their good favor for the long haul was vital. My motive was not entirely altruistic. I intended to remain in business indefinitely. If an Allen organ was ever traded in, I wanted to be sure it would be traded in on a new Allen. Also, I knew that new organs are often sold upon the recommendation of current owners; therefore, I wanted to make sure that the owners of Allen organs would recommend Allen Organ Company to other prospective customers.

I can't say that these "policies" and "philosophies" were part of some carefully designed "grand plan" for success. They just "felt" right to me. In retrospect, I must say that ideals such as craftsmanship, quality, loyalty, honesty, and permanent values were very much a part of the predominantly Pennsylvania German culture of the Allentown area. Undoubtedly, I was influenced by a long exposure to this culture and the people who lived by its ideals. Happily, many of these people joined Allen Organ Company and helped establish our reputation for excellence.

Of course, just "wanting" to be excellent was not enough to make it so. I learned that running a company is like paddling a canoe upstream—it takes a lot of effort just to stay where you already are. There were always bills to be paid, new customers to be found, proper equipment to be bought and kept in repair, and adequate factory space to be obtained. We had gotten upstream "a ways," but I sensed we could quickly be swept back if we were the least bit complacent. During these formative years, the Company was a partially successful enterprise—successful in that sales were increasing each year but hardly profitable. In fact, during this period I had to, once again, solicit financial support from outside the Company. Luckily, several local individuals were willing to invest in a still fledgling yet promising Company.

As far as finding new customers, I knew even in 1946 that we would have to look beyond the local area. At that time, the standard method of selling musical instruments was through dealers. Therefore, ads were placed in the appropriate trade magazines, and we started to build a dealer network which began with three or four dealers. During this time period another important event occurred in the life of the Company. Sometime in 1946, we sold an Allen organ to an organist by the name of Robert Pearce. He was working as a free lance entertainer at the time but had a broad interest in the organ field. At some point during one of his visits to the factory, the idea of his joining the Company arose. In 1947, Robert Pearce became an employee, serving as a combination salesman/demonstrator/fixer. Since then, he has put in many years with the Company making sales, teaching, working with customers, and establishing an outstanding sales and dealer organization. As the Company grew, he became Vice President of Sales, a position which he still holds today.

In those days our competition—besides pipe organs—was, of course, the popular Hammond as well as some newcomers into the "non-pipe" field. Conn, Baldwin, and Wurlitzer all began producing competing instruments. I quickly learned that I could not rest on my laurels given the "all is fair" mentality of the business world. I realized that I had better hang on to the innovative spirit which got the whole thing going in the first place. If I didn't, I knew the competitors would have no qualms about invading our turf.

Fortunately, I was not only able just to hang on to my innovative spirit, I became rather adept at it. I don't mean to imply that this was only a one man show, but I did continue to make direct, innovative contributions to the art of electronic organ building. However, perhaps more importantly, I developed an ability to sense and to promote innovation in others within the Company. I always kept an open mind to new ideas— even some radical ideas from outside the Company. I didn't know it at that time, but I was destined to play a key role in the birth and growth of one of the most significant innovations in the history of organ building—the Digital Computer Organ. If I had not been able to maintain my innovative spirit through the years, I probably would have "missed the boat" in foreseeing the impact of that momentous development and would have unwisely rejected it. I will expand on that story later. At any rate, Allen held its own over the years against stiff competition—on the strength of its innovation as well as its reputation for uncompromising sound quality, superior construction, and permanence of service.

When I looked outside the factory at 8th and Pittston Streets in late 1952, I saw knots of congestion in all directions. I knew that if the Company was going to break through into profitability, we would have to sell more organs—which I thought was possible. However, if we sold more organs, I could not see how we would be able to build them efficiently in the cramped quarters we were then leasing. We only leased a portion of the building and had to share such things as parking space and the loading dock with the other lessees. This added to the frustration and further reduced efficiency.

As I pondered this situation, I also began to consider a vacant textile plant for sale in Macungie, a small town several miles southwest of Allentown. We needed more room, and there it was. By early 1953, we had taken the plunge, had purchased the 25,000 square foot plant in Macungie, and were moving in immediately. After all the financial details were ironed out, the mortgage payments actually weren't too different from what we were paying to lease the smaller facility at 10th and Pittston. However, the much larger Macungie plant seemed luxuriously spacious—at least for a while.

Electronic assembly area of the Macungie plant—1953.

At this point, seven years had passed since I resumed my organ venture back in 1945. There were many ups and downs during these years, and I had learned a great deal about business and the art of running a company. But by 1953, I was finally beginning to feel that true viability had been achieved—profitability was occurring and the Allen Organ Company was here to stay.

On a personal note, in early 1949, I was married to Martha, and by 1958, had four children, Marc, Steven, Sandra, and Judith. Steven, especially, became interested in the affairs of Allen Organ at an early age and became active in the company upon his graduation from Penn State University in 1975. And, in 1964, I purchased a farm which subsequently became my "second business."

Moving
Along

In trying to characterize the time period from 1953 to 1961 in the life of the Company, I would call it a stable time marked by steady growth. Actually, Allen Organ Company was a minor player at that time. Other companies such as Hammond, Conn, Baldwin, and Wurlitzer had well-established names. In order to compete and grow, we had to do "our thing" better than the other guys. We "felt" our way regarding the specifics. However, the basic policies and principles which were learned in the prior years still formed the foundation for our philosophy of operation—no layoffs occurred, the products were built to last, and the organs sounded and acted more like pipe organs than any other non-pipe instruments. We were not only leaders in technological innovation but also kept our productivity high by hiring good people and judiciously expanding and improving our physical plant.

We were also set apart from our competition in the early years because of another important difference. Allen Organ Company catered to the individual needs of its customers, whereas our competitors tended to think more in terms of standard "off-the-shelf" products. For example, as far back as 1947, we built the world's first three-manual electronic organ because that was what the customer wanted. Incidentally, that organ went to St. Paul's Lutheran Church in Catasauqua, Pennsylvania, and served them for thirty-three years; it was replaced with a new Allen in 1980. We even went on to build four-manual electronic organs. The other companies seemed to exclusively produce the smaller two-manual organs first popularized by Hammond. We also built the smaller two-manual organs, but we continued to emulate pipe organs as I had done from the very beginning. For those seeking an institutional organ, as opposed to a home organ, Allen offered a tempting alternative to a pipe organ. The customer could get an instrument that had a standard pipe organ console. It played like a pipe organ and sounded much like a pipe organ; but it cost much less and produced fewer problems than a pipe organ. It's certainly true that we constantly came up against the prejudice of purists—sometimes but not always the organist—regarding anything "electronic." However, for many churches on tight budgets, we offered the best alternative to a "real" pipe organ. In these cases, it was a choice between an Allen Organ or no organ at all, given the realities of the economics involved.

Obviously, a lot of work went into building the Company from 1953 to 1961. Because space does not permit a lengthy recitation of everything that happened during those years, I will only touch on some random highlights—humorous, technological, marketing—to give the reader a flavor of that time period.

Mr. and Mrs. Harold Steinbright of Cedars, Pennsylvania, traded their Allen "Original Organ" of 1945 on a new Allen.

One of the important technical developments which influenced this time frame was the "Gyrophonic Projector." I developed and patented this rotating

Front and rear views of a gyrophonic speaker cabinet—1960.

speaker system around 1949 in order to add a "liveliness" to the sound of the electronically generated pipe tones. The Gyrophonic Projector was a big success. Organ experts such as Dr. William H. Barnes lauded the development. Dealers and customers were favorably impressed. Competitors, caught off guard, were rather creative in quickly dreaming up "problems" connected with the "Gyro." The "Gyro" supposedly "induced nausea" because of "motion fatigue." The "Gyro" somehow interfered with the heating system of the church, which in turn caused numerous head colds in the choir. However, in spite of these initial attacks, many competitors soon followed suit and offered some form of "speakers-in-motion" arrangement themselves.

Aside from the improvement made in the sound, the Gyrophonic Projector could be turned on and off by the organist. This deceptively insignificant fact is really very important, for I learned long ago that people of all levels of expertise can't "remember" the subtleties of different sounds for more than a brief time. Having a tonal-improvement feature which can be turned on and off is a great way to get around this difficulty. Listeners can easily perceive the improvement because they don't have to retain any of the different sounds in their memories very long. Turning the effect on and off gives a relatively instantaneous comparison—with no "remembering" involved.

A related situation exists when people are required to choose from among several different organ manufacturers and/or models. We found that doing side-by-side demonstrations was a good way to alleviate the "remembering" problem. Again, listeners could get relative comparisons instantaneously if the two organs being compared were sitting side-by-side. Allen consistently won most of these side-by-side demonstrations, including an "international" side-by-side held in 1956, where we competed against a European rival.

Furthermore, a fascinating sidelight to the Gyrophonic Projector story exists. Early in the development of the system, I was searching for a quiet, multiple-speed, AC motor to turn the speaker assembly. I asked Century Electric Company, a motor manufacturer, whether they could build such a motor. Well, they could. However, more importantly, Fred Pillsbury, President of Century Electric, was an avid organ buff. When Mr. Pillsbury learned about our project, he quickly became personally involved. He later became a stockholder in Allen Organ Company; and, until his death in 1988, he was an Allen director. His continuing support and philanthropic activities in the church organ field were deeply appreciated by all of us in the organ community.

In 1953, St. Catharine of Siena Roman Catholic Church, in Allentown, bought their second Allen Organ for use in their new cathedral, which was built next to the original church. In the same year Allen Organ introduced the S-12. The low-priced S-12 model sold for $1666; it not only attracted substantial attention in the marketplace but many individuals were buying S-12s for their homes. This was Allen's first foray into the home market as distinguished from the institutional market, our traditional forte. As a result, many new dealers were added; and, by the end of the year, Allen Organ Company was a very busy place.

By 1954, we again ran out of space and decided to add 10,000 square feet to the factory. At the same time, our employment increased to 130. The pent-up demand caused by the War was being released; sales increased accordingly. People were on the move building new communities and new churches. Confidence in the future was high. New models included the successful C-2—an instrument that offered a "large organ tone" and was completely self-contained.

The "Organette" appeared in 1955. This was a spinet organ for the home market. The Organette evolved over the following years as we responded to the desires of the market. We even decorated some of these models with rather elaborate hand-painted designs which were very much in vogue at that time.

Perhaps we were a little bit ahead of our time in the use of innovative marketing tools. We came up with an automatic organ demonstrator called "AREOS," which stands for "Allen's Robot Electronic Organ Salesman." The demonstration organ "played" organ music all by itself while a recording of a salesman extolled the virtues of the instrument to people curious enough to listen.

When I see similar kinds of sales tools being used today, I wonder whether we retired AREOS too soon.

Also, in 1955, we were talking about having the world's largest electronic organ for demonstrations at the factory. This behemoth was equipped with 32 foot stops, a rare luxury in those days. Only the largest pipe organs had 32 foot pipes because of their immense size. Our electronic version was much smaller. I recall feeling self-satisfaction when we received an order for an Allen electronic 32 foot organ to augment the pipe organ going into the Lehigh University Chapel in Bethlehem, Pennsylvania.

In that same year, our Sales Manager, Robert Pearce, appeared on a popular television show, Bob Considine's "Cavalcade of Progress." It featured a tour of the factory and a description of our products. Toward the end of the year, 200 employees and guests attended the Allen Fall Festival. In addition, the new Allen logo appeared nationwide in an advertisement in *Life* magazine's special issue on religion.

In October, 1956, our staff was augmented by Lawrence Phelps, who had already achieved a substantial reputation within the pipe organ industry as a designer and student of the pipe organ. Mr. Phelps had a tremendous insight into the nature of sound as produced by pipe organs and was able to provide valuable inputs during his tenure at Allen Organ Company. Regretfully, in October, 1957, he decided to pursue his career elsewhere. (He was to return to our employ in 1982). I suspected that he was unsatisfied with the best sounds we could produce at that time. However, he never specifically indicated this. Following his departure and sensing his dissatisfaction, as well as my own, I began to zero in on possible characteristics of pipe organs which might be missing from the instruments that we were producing at that time.

By 1956, our cabinet shop had its own building—a 31,000 square foot extension of the main plant. The introduction of a special exhaust system took care of most of the sawdust more efficiently. Our purchase of twelve more adjoining acres indicated the success and optimism we were enjoying. The Company's first sales seminar was held the last week in January of that year; participants heard me proclaim that, technologically, Allen intended to stay ten years ahead of others in the electronic organ field.

Later that year, an Allen Organ was used at the American Guild of Organists' convention with a special event held in the Lewisohn Stadium in New York City. Of course, installing a "real" pipe organ inside the stadium just to entertain this stronghold of "purists" was out of the question. They had to "settle" for the next best thing, an Allen. Much to my great satisfaction, the organ received excellent reviews.

Further, the prestigious Philadelphia Orchestra discovered the effectiveness of an Allen Organ in 1957. The Orchestra used an Allen Organ in a special performance at the Academy of Music that year. We later received a letter from Eugene Ormandy praising "this wonderful instrument." A continent away, a technical article written by me appeared in the British journal, *Electronic Engineering*. This all helped our own prestige.

We were on the move—sales in 1958 were up over 1957 despite a recession, and 12,000 more square feet were added to the factory. Church installations continued to be the mainstay of our business, but we were also acquiring a few fans from other arenas. For example, Jackie Gleason had a rather large, unusual, round house built near Peekskill, New York. An Allen Organette was incorporated into Gleason's custom-built office directly behind his chair so that he could instantly try out his musical inspirations just by turning around and playing.

In a different musical circle, conductor Leopold Stokowski commissioned Allen to design and build a new instrument for his orchestra, the Houston Symphony. He believed that orchestras were fundamentally weak in the bass and wanted an instrument of two-and-one-half octaves, with a small keyboard, which would play the same tones as the double basses but with much more power at the very low frequencies. "I believe that in time it would be an important instrument in every orchestra in the world," Stokowski wrote, "but of course at first it would receive the usual resistance to new ideas." To date he was wrong about the first part of his prediction. His Allen bass is still one of a kind.

Following up on a promise I made to our dealers three years earlier about staying ten years ahead technologically, Allen Organ Company went "solid-state" in 1959; we announced that the Company would no longer build vacuum tube generators. Instead, after three years of development, the new tone generators would be completely transistorized. Many of our competitors were caught off guard, so we enjoyed a technological edge for awhile. Overall, the Company continued to build respect—financially, technically, and in customer satisfaction. In the Allen *Organews* that year, the question was raised, "What organist of renown will be willing to play an electronic organ, even if it is the finest in its field?" This alludes to an issue of great importance even to this day, the "purist's" attitude toward non-pipe organs and the influence this has on the organ community in general. I'll have more to say on this subject later.

In 1959, the *Organews* addressed the above question by citing several upcoming recitals to be performed on Allen installations by internationally famous organists. The organists mentioned were David Craighead, Organ Department Chairman of the Eastman School, Rochester, New York; Pierre Cochereau, world-famous organist of the Cathedral of Notre Dame, Paris, France; and, of course, Virgil Fox, organist of the Riverside Church of New York City.

Also in 1959, the Company established a retirement trust for salaried employees. Sales for 1959 were 10% ahead of 1958 with a large backlog at the end of the year.

In 1960, a record number (143) attended our now-established annual sales seminar. The electronic harpsichord was introduced, and the solid-state tone generators were a solid success. The fourth major expansion to the Macungie factory was begun—30,000 additional square feet were added to house the Final Test area. This is the addition upon which was erected the mammoth "Allen Organs" logo, which still unfailingly catches the eyes of visitors as they approach the factory. An Allen C-1 found its way to Kwassui Junior College, Nagasaki, Japan. And, according to the records, in 1960 an Allen TC-1 accompanied a 3300 voice choir at the Festival of Music in Princeton, New Jersey.

Another good year occurred in 1961. We had about 75 dealers on board by then and the solid-state Allen Organs were selling well. Lawrence Welk ordered an Allen electronic harpsichord which was subsequently used on his popular TV program. Around the same time, we tried to branch out a bit by offering custom stereo units, but had little success in that particular area.

By this time, I had spent countless hours listening to organ pipes in order to understand the subtle differences between the sound coming from an organ pipe and the sound coming from my electronic tone generator. I became convinced that one important element missing from my electronic tone generator was what I came to call "random motion." I had never seen anything specifically describing this phenomenon in print. However, it was clear to me that organ pipes and, in fact, all other acoustic instruments exhibit minute, yet continuous, random variations in pitch and intensity. In contrast, my electronic tone generator, at that point, exhibited a very steady, static sound. Of course, the Gyrophonic Projector helped provide some of the missing motion to the sound of the electronic tone generator. However, the Gyrophonic Projector produced a steady, repetitive undulation in the pitch and intensity of the sound suggesting a vibrato or tremolo effect.

The random motion I sought had a much different character—a kind of nervous unsteadiness. I finally was able to produce the sound I was after by powering the tone generators from a special power supply which created a randomly-varying voltage output. Use of this power supply in conjunction with a new circuit arrangement greatly improved our sound; the technique was patented. "Electronic Whind," a term coined by Robert Pearce to describe the effect, became an important feature of the Allen Organ. Our customers liked the natural sound of "Electronic Whind." But some of our competitors tried to minimize the development. One said that they were "not interested in imitating the defects of the pipe organ." Another tried to frighten customers with rumors about Allen's "unstable power supplies." Eventually, however, many of these competitors began offering their own versions of "Electronic Whind."

As an indicator of our progress to that point in time, I note that, in 1961, the Allen Organ Company became a public corporation; on November 1 of that year the first offering of stock was made available to the general public. Almost overnight, Allen Organ Company was owned not merely by the original investors and management but also by approximately 500 additional investors.

Hi-Tech
Stirrings

An interesting phenomenon that I noticed while listening to organ pipes and most other instruments— perhaps the most outstanding example is the violin— was that the musical sounds were accompanied by a small amount of "noise." I was recently visited by a young lady from academe who was both a violinist and a physicist. During the course of the conversation I mentioned that one of the components of violin sound is noise, and she seemed to recoil at the thought. Nevertheless, a small amount of noise is a component of many musical sounds, including that of organ pipes. Over the years this fact has become increasingly acknowledged by acousticians and others interested in the production of musical sounds.

During the 1960s, we learned that organ prospects could indeed perceive these subtle sound characteristics when properly demonstrated. Interestingly, even with this arsenal of demonstrations, I encountered many well-seasoned organists who summarily rejected the idea that organ pipes, in fact, include random motion components as part of their sound. Clear demonstrations of this phenomenon to such persons were usually non-productive in that many of these organ "experts", once taking a position, found it hard to back off from that position regardless of the "proof of the pudding."

Another element of musical sound which I probed during those years was an effect sometimes called "chiff." It has become clear to students of musical sounds, over the years, that many musical instruments sound different at the onset of their sound production as compared to the steady-state condition which follows. For example, a violinist can bow the string of the violin in an accented fashion at the beginning of the sound, resulting in an easily perceived articulation of the tone, and then settle down into a more steady bowing during the aftersound. I observed that organ pipes have a similar effect in that some would begin with a slight "explosion" of sound—and noise—and then settle down to a more even, steady sound.

On June 27, 1961, I was granted U. S. Patents 2,989,886 and 2,989,887 covering mechanisms to produce chiff, random motion and noise in conjunction with the production of electronic organ sounds. On June 5, 1962, I was granted U. S. Patent 3,037,413 covering another method for production of chiff and similar transient effects in electronic organs.

To dwell a bit on the subject of inventing, I was happy to be a co-inventor with engineer Milton Nelson in the development of the photocell expression system described in U. S. Patent 3,045,522. Up to that time the volume control systems for electronic organs were basically rheostats or variable resistors. These devices invariably became noisy after a time, causing static-like sounds to emanate from the loudspeakers. The photoelectric system eliminated these noises. Moreover, reliability was dramatically improved. Most companies adopted this system in the years that followed.

There was substantial, technological growth in the country in the decade from 1960-1970. Generally speaking, confidence in "technology" was high and innovation was flourishing. For example, during this period, the space program was in high gear; each new space development was eagerly followed by people all over the world. During this period, the integrated circuit became a reality, including the ubiquitous TTL devices which came onto the market during this time. The first commercial communications satellite was launched. IBM developed its famous System/360 and the BASIC computer language was created. These examples are just a few that reflect the quality of many of the technological developments which took place then. Moreover, many of these technological innovations are still quite relevant today more than twenty years after their development.

In contrast to other fields, I believe the musical instrument industry was slow to join the technological bandwagon. In Allen Organ's situation, although we did indeed come up with significant improvements as described above, we were essentially building electronic organs as we had in the past. We had a proven formula for success based on high quality, customer satisfaction, fiscal prudence, and the electronic oscillator. Why change?

Well, at first, it appeared we really didn't have to make fundamental changes. Sales were steadily increasing, at least in the early 1960s. Acceptance of the Allen electronic organ as a good alternative to a pipe organ was increasing. In fact, much of the history of the time period deals with prestigious installations and events which brought Allen into the limelight more than ever. The Company was still expanding with an employee roster of over 600. Our success during this period was due more to our continued hard work than to any major technological breakthroughs. The only problem with this was the fact that our competitors were slowly becoming more of a factor in the marketplace. This showed up when our sales growth flattened toward the end of the decade. I sensed that maintaining our leadership in the organ field would become more and more difficult if we simply continued down the same path. However, I didn't have the answer to this dilemma—at least, not immediately.

At that time, our competition had basically two strategies. One was to try to compete with us on our own turf—the institutional organ market—by emulating our earlier move into transistorization. The other was to create a new market—the "easy-play" home organ market—based on simple, low-cost tone generation combined with all kinds of automatic playing features. The companies who chose to follow the easy-play route did so because this method was an easy way to sell organs at the time. These companies were indeed selling many organs; however, they were also planting the seeds of their own destruction.

Even though a major, organ-related, technological development did occur in the late 1960s, I'll deal with that in the following chapters. For now, this chapter will focus on some more reminiscing about the Allen "electronic" organ. Accordingly I will reveal some more highlights of the decade.

Lincoln Center planned to open its first building, Philharmonic Hall, with a gala concert on September 23, 1962. A pipe organ was being incorporated into the building. Several scores requiring an organ were part of the musical program. As the big day drew near, it became clear that the pipe organ would not be finished in time. A committee, including Leonard Bernstein and William Schuman, was hastily assembled to address the problem. They decided to use an Allen Organ to save the program. We were asked to install a suitable instrument on a temporary basis with one-week's notice.

This would normally be a six-to-eight week job, but I was not about to miss this fabulous opportunity. We quickly agreed to the Committee's request and told them not to worry. Allen would be there ready for the opening day. We brought in a moderately-sized, two-manual organ with enough power to compete with the large symphony orchestra. Working around the clock in the midst of a din of construction noise, the Allen was brought to life just in time for the rehearsal.

In recognition of Allen's contribution to the program, my wife and I received an invitation to Opening Night, a very formal, white-tie affair. We attended along with many luminaries such as First Lady Jacqueline Kennedy, Governor Nelson Rockefeller, and Adlai Stevenson. As we settled into our seats in anticipation of the start of the concert, the first sound we heard was that of the Allen Organ, played by perhaps the most famous organist of that time, E. Power Biggs. On the program were the Gloria from Beethoven's "Missa Solemnis" and the first part of Mahler's gigantic Eighth Symphony, conducted by Leonard Bernstein.

As The *Morning Call* of Allentown reported: "The Allen Organ, installed hastily by the Macungie company's technicians at the request of an organ committee from Lincoln Center, was as capable of filling its role as the great pipe organ which will eventually take its place....The organ made itself known with the opening 'Star Spangled Banner'; brought a cathedral sound to the Beethoven 'Gloria,' and contributed with extraordinary effect to the tremendous Mahler score."

In the weeks following Opening Night, several other concerts were held which included prominent works for both organ and orchestra. Columbia Records was present; they later released recordings of the various performances. The publicity surrounding these events certainly enhanced Allen's image as a builder of fine institutional organs. A concert held a few weeks after Opening Night featured the Philadelphia Orchestra under Eugene Ormandy with E. Power Biggs as organ soloist. The *New York Herald Tribune*, reporting about the substitution of an Allen for the Aeolian-Skinner pipe organ, observed that "the switch brought pain to many an organ purist, but all we've got to say is that Aeolian-Skinner had better look to its laurels when Allen transistorized oscillators are around. The pipe-less stand-in had good definition of sound in both reeds and strings, and it even managed the 'chiff' at the beginning of each sound on the flute stops, which is so highly prized by devotees of the now fashionable Baroque organ." Dear Reader, I couldn't have summed it up any better.

Unfortunately, establishing and keeping a good image is not merely a matter of doing a good job. In the very same year we "proved" ourselves at Lincoln Center, someone started a rumor that transistorized organs would be damaged by radioactive fallout. This was nonsense, but someone apparently wanted to attack the "image" of the electronic organ by capitalizing on the public's legitimate fear of radiation fallout. Happily, the vast majority saw through this particular ruse. Sadly, though, this kind of tactic is all too common in our business. Moreover, much of it is subtle—not as overt and obviously ludicrous as the example just cited.

As a postscript to the Lincoln Center story, some years later we were again approached by Lincoln Center to help solve a problem. They were getting complaints about poor acoustics; some experts attributed part of the problem to the pipe organ—the one that didn't work for Opening Night. Well, the pipe organ was removed, the hall was renovated, and upon reopening sported a new name, Avery Fisher Hall. The management of Lincoln Center rented Allens for awhile, were pleased with the results, and decided to go with a permanent Allen installation. They gave us another call—this time with a purchase order.

The use of Allen Organs to accompany symphony orchestras became more common after the great success at Lincoln Center. An amusing anecdote connected with such a concert occurred when Robert Pearce and I decided to personally supervise the placement and voicing of the organ to be used to accompany the Philadelphia Orchestra in a recording of "Thus Spake Zarathustra" by Richard Strauss. The recording session was scheduled for a Sunday morning at 10:00 A.M. Having set up the organ the day before, we relaxed Sunday morning and waited to enjoy the performance.

Well, when the full organ was sounded with the orchestra, an unmistakable out-of-tuneness was heard. Much to our dismay, we learned that the Orchestra was using a non-standard A-442 pitch reference; we had tuned the organ to the standard A-440. As I recall, Mr. Ormandy naturally assumed that retuning the organ was out of the question and the session would have to be cancelled—at considerable expense. Keeping my fingers crossed because of time pressure, I decided to try for a retuning of the organ while the orchestra ran through some other music. Robert Pearce and I disconnected the organ, raced it to another room, and worked feverishly to change the pitch to A-442. In a little over an hour, we had the organ back with the orchestra and ready to go. Mr. Ormandy smiled his approval and conducted a marvelous performance.

In 1963, the Sales Seminar was held in our newly built showrooms which had been added to the factory the year before. The Theatre Compact model was introduced at the seminar.

The following year, 1964, another 66,000 square feet of factory space was added. This was used for assembly and finishing. Now our employee count topped 600. In addition, we went "international" with the establishment of a dealership in Switzerland.

With regard to interesting installations, we had a few that year including a specially built organ for the chapel in the Church Center for United Nations in New York City. An Allen was also installed on the aircraft carrier, U.S.S. Champlain, the same ship that retrieved Alan Shepard after his descent from outer space.

We suffered a personal loss in 1965 with the death of Michale M. MyLymuk. His contributions to the Company were many, going back to the 1940s. Eugene Moroz, who also had a great deal of experience with the Company, having joined in 1946, was named Vice-President of Production.

In 1966, over 200 dealers attended our sales seminar. Our staff was surprised at the large surge of new orders, this just following months of heavy ordering. As a result, the backlog required working on Saturday mornings, skipping vacations, and carefully using temporary help.

Facing the need to expand again, we decided to establish a subsidiary operation, Rocky Mount Instruments (RMI), in Rocky Mount, North Carolina, where land was inexpensive and labor plentiful. We announced our plans in 1966 and set up a temporary 10,000-square-foot operation in an empty tobacco warehouse. By the following year, we moved to a handsome, 60,000-square-foot, newly-built factory located in a nearby rural area. Many new products geared to the popular market and carrying the RMI label were designed. RMI portable keyboards, novelty instruments, and portable amplifiers were introduced. We developed a rapport with many popular and rock musicians of the day. RMI's mascot, "Gopher Baroque," provided the "Underground Sound" in vogue at the time. Actually, many musicians are still fond of their vintage RMI equipment and still use it today.

The Doors used an RMI "Rock-si-chord" in their hit song, "Hello, I Love You." The Rock-si-chord was a combination harpsichord and guitar played from a keyboard. Other top musicians and groups of the day such as Hank Williams, Jr., Deep Purple, The Association, Frank Zappa, and The Beach Boys, adopted the Rock-si-chord's successor, the RMI "Electra Piano and Harpsichord."

Formal dedication of the Rocky Mount plant was held in 1967 with North Carolina Governor, Dan K. Moore, cutting the ribbon. The employee count at RMI had grown to about 100 people by then. Meanwhile, back in Macungie, an April sales seminar brought in about 250 dealers. The Carousel Model was introduced. This instrument, aimed at the home market, offered many popular sounds including a rather convincing strumming-string section all in one package. Moreover, Allens continued to be used in concert with orchestras, including a performance by the National Symphony Orchestra at the huge Washington National Cathedral.

In 1968, organists Earl Ness and William Whitehead performed a two-organ recital at the Drayton Avenue Presbyterian Church in Ferndale, Michigan. A three-manual Allen was used with a large Moller pipe organ. Organ concerts featuring two organs playing simultaneously are quite rare; however, there are some scores available for two organs. The organists in this recital had been recorded at a similar performance in Philadelphia a few years earlier; the results were quite satisfying both musically and with regard to Allen's prestige. On the popular front, when Steve Allen went shopping for an organ in 1968, guess what he bought? Of course, he selected an Allen.

In an effort to diversify in 1969, we bought another company, Eichler Wood Products, Inc., a manufacturer of pallets, shipping containers, etc. Eichler operated as an Allen subsidiary for a while, but we were not satisfied, so we sold it in 1971. At the January 1969 sales seminar, we announced the Crystal Carousel and Continental Carousel derived from the original Carousel model. Also, in 1969, we announced that Allen Organ was involved in a joint program with a large aerospace company. The announcement only hinted at what was occurring. There certainly was a lot "going on," but I'll tackle that issue a little later.

By 1970, Allen Organs were to be found on six of the seven continents. An Allen Classic organ was purchased for the one-thousand seat Alice Tully Hall of Lincoln Center. Jackie Gleason bought an Allen Carousel. However, closer to home, Allen delivered what was undoubtedly the largest electronic organ of its kind in the world to the Tenth Presbyterian Church in Philadelphia. Dr. Robert Elmore, the noted concert organist and composer who was Director of Music and organist at the church at the time, had requested the custom, four-manual, 132-stop Allen. Purists were aghast that Elmore, the organist's organist, chose an electronic organ. But his reasoning made perfect sense. He explained that, with the funds and space available, he could either settle for a rather "modest two-manual pipe organ" or get an organ with the resources to match his broad creative interests. Happily, he chose the latter.

Finally, at the close of this time period, Allen announced a new capture system based on something called "microelectronics." The capture system of an organ memorizes or "captures" the various combinations of stops used by an organist during a particular performance. The organist sets up and captures the desired combinations before the performance. Once captured, a particular combination of stops on the organ, often involving numerous physical changes to the pattern of stops, may be brought back instantly at

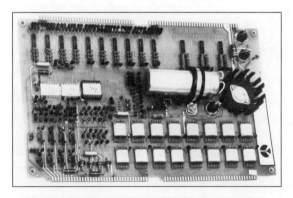

Rockwell–designed and built capture system for
stop control of an Allen console—the first
"microelectronics" application to a musical instrument—1970.

the push of a single button. Early capture systems were built using relays and involved rather bulky systems of hardware. In contrast, the new capture system did not need relays and was physically small. Most who pondered this new curiosity at the time didn't know they were actually previewing an incredible new era about to begin. Only a very few people knew about the immensely significant events taking place behind the scenes. However, much more was about to be announced in 1971.

Virgil Fox

As Allen Organ continued to build upon its innovation, growth, and reputation during the 1960s and 1970s, we occasionally crossed paths with one of the world's top organists—Virgil Fox.

Mr. Fox played recitals on Allen Organs during this period. Subsequently, he made periodic visits to our factory. I remember how vibrant and "bigger than life" he was—filled with ideas and dreams. During this time, he dropped enough hints that I'm quite sure he wanted us to "loan" him an Allen Organ. He was dreaming about going on tour with a "portable" organ. He wanted to bring the organ to the people in a non-conventional, dramatic way. I just couldn't give in to his wish to have a permanent Allen "loaner" organ. I was concerned that such a special arrangement would be perceived as being contrived—as though we were trying to "buy" Fox's endorsement. So, during the 1960s and early 1970s, we had to be satisfied with occasional keep-in-touch visits. It wasn't until 1976, that we became more closely associated with this outstanding performer.

Virgil Fox did, of course, become a "touring" organist. During the late 1960s and into the 1970s, he toured using an electronic organ from another company which, I believe, he rented or borrowed. He popularized much of the organ literature as he appeared at colleges, theaters, churches, music halls, and "rock palaces" occasionally. He was especially interested in appealing to young people; therefore, he developed his "act" with this in mind. His young audience wanted light shows and smoke bombs, and that's exactly what he gave them in addition to his superb organ playing. To say he was unique is an understatement. For his efforts, he was rewarded with an army of loyal, vocally-appreciative supporters.

In 1976, Virgil Fox decided to buy his own touring organ and chose a new digital computer instrument from Allen. The organ was to include an imposing, four-manual console which was hardly portable. Yet, virtuoso Fox felt he needed this weighty console to achieve the proper effect at his concerts. He was very much a part of the design team from the beginning. I recall many a late-evening telephone call from Virgil Fox during the construction of the organ. We chatted about his most recent ideas for enhancing the success of the instrument. These conversations were always stimulating because of the boundless excitement and enthusiasm in his voice. This enthusiasm rubbed off on all of us working on the project. Someone came up with the idea of designing a special stop just for him. We secretly installed this special stop on the organ and revealed it to him at the appropriate time. It was called the "Fox Humana." He was delighted.

As Virgil Fox's organ neared completion, we realized that the instrument would be of interest to the dealers who would be attending the upcoming 1977 sales seminar. I asked Mr. Fox how he felt about our showing the new instrument to our dealers. He was not only enthusiastic about it but he wanted to participate. So, we set up the organ in a remote place in the factory. We wanted to surprise everybody. We didn't tell anyone that Virgil Fox was personally going to demonstrate the organ at the Seminar. At the appointed hour during the Seminar, we ushered the dealers into the factory in front of the draped console. Shortly thereafter we unveiled the Virgil Fox touring organ to the approving applause from our audience. As we pretended to begin the demonstration, Virgil Fox came stomping in shouting, "Don't touch that organ! It's mine!" There was an instant eruption of cheers at the sight of Fox himself racing down the aisle to claim the keys and stops of his very own touring organ. It was a moment few organ enthusiasts could ever forget.

With his new Allen Organ, Virgil Fox gave his first public concert on October 1, 1977, at Hackensack High

School in New Jersey. In the next few years, until his untimely death on October 25, 1980, he gave at least sixty performances on his travelling Allen. He played wherever people wanted to hear him—Macomb, Illinois; Saranac Lake, New York; Wolf Trap; Academy of Music in Philadelphia; Washington, D.C.; Brooklyn College; Saratoga, New York; and Victoria, Texas, to name a few.

Fox used a special truck to transport the organ to his many concert sites. On one of these trips, the truck was involved in a bad accident in New Mexico. Let's let Virgil tell us about it himself by referring to the following replication of a letter I received from him about the incident.

Virgil Fox

CASA LAGOMAR
9 LAGOMAR ROAD
PALM BEACH, FLORIDA 33480
(305) 655-2775

May 28, 1980

Mr. Jerome Markowitz
Allen Organ Company
Macungie, Pa. 18062

Dear Jerome:

Although it has been our policy, because of my position as a concert organist playing all makes of instruments, to never endorse an organ (even though I own one), I feel that I must write to you now and share our feelings about the incredible experience we endured several weeks ago.

As I related to you on the telephone, our touring organ that you so beautifully custom made for me was enroute to a performance in San Antonio. A driver pulled onto the road in front of our truck in Lordsburg, New Mexico, sending it down and into the ditch.

We were shocked and frightened to learn that the truck had rolled over and we anticipated the worst when we heard that the technician had been pinned inside for nearly an hour with gasoline pouring in on him as the vehicle lay upside down on its roof. The windshield was removed by a passerby and in due course he was rescued, shaken but otherwise unhurt.

The truck was completely destroyed and we expected that that would be the same story with the organ.

The organ was ultimately loaded into a U-Haul truck and brought to San Antonio where we waited for it on stage. After taking stock of the damage that was visible, we hesitatingly connected everything up and were delighted beyond all possible imagination when the instrument actually played without any trouble.

Jerome, this is nothing short of a near miracle when one considers that the console and computer sections came to rest in the wreck in an upside down position with the keyboards hanging free and the stop jams knocked out of alignment. I thought computers were delicate!

While we would like to take a portion of the credit for the fact that the instrument survived the crash inasmuch as we requested from the Allen Organ Company that they take certain steps in the building of this instrument to make it more durable for touring, we must, however, say that the end result of surviving this crash comes to bear upon the fact that it was designed and built superbly.

I would also like to tell you that I am pleased as I travel about the country and have exposure to other Allen products, as I have seen the same care and attention going into these instruments that has been incorporated into mine. Although I would like to believe I was given preferred treatment at the Allen Organ Company with regards to workmanship, I have come to appreciate the fact that the same quality seems to go into every instrument although I would not recommend every owner of an Allen Organ run it through a truck wreck to bear this fact out.

You are to be congratulated, Jerome, as well as all the technicians who worked on my instrument and I must say that the organ has truly passed the "touring organ" test in respect to both tone quality and dependability. The computer tone generation system of the instrument has been an enormous asset to the successful production of our concerts.

We never cease to be approached at all concerts by people who are delighted with my choice of organs, specifically the Allen, for our touring instrument. It is a joy to play. The state-of-the-art reverberation systems, digital delay and the voicing techniques that you have employed provide us with a continued spirit of adventure as we move from one auditorium to another.

Nevertheless without meaning to get off the track, I wish to again tell you that I am still in a state of amazement and joy realizing that this great instrument, which has been seen by so many people and enjoyed by so many could, after three years on the road come right through such a calamity, although dusty and bruised, working perfectly suitable for a concert.

I want to tell you [and] all those who worked on this organ because most certainly your company deserves the credit for building such a wonderful organ for me.

Warmest regards as always,

/s/ Virgil

Virgil Fox

P. S. Feel free to use this letter.

cc: Virgil Fox Society

I got to know Virgil Fox on a first-name basis during his visits. On one occasion he even came to my home to practice. He was scheduled to give a concert in our area and needed an organ for practice in the late evening hours. He called me asking to use the organ in my home, which was amenable to me. I remember that after he finished practicing, we had the most marvelous discussion covering many diverse topics. What a walking bundle of enthusiasm!

As far back as 1976 when Virgil and I were discussing the possibility of our building his touring organ, I sensed that he was afflicted with some kind of ailment. However, I did not know what it was or how serious it might be. Nevertheless, he seemed to be performing quite admirably. However, watching him over the following few years gave me the feeling that his illness was getting progressively worse. We later learned that he had cancer. He phoned me at home one evening in early 1980. As I was away at the time, he spoke to my wife, Martha. Virgil asked her whether she knew of anyone or anything that might give him some hope in battling this terrible disease. This was a very difficult, sobering conversation, indeed.

Our staff and I derived much satisfaction from our experiences and meetings with Virgil Fox. We were all profoundly saddened when this colorful artist died in the Fall, 1980.

Virgil Fox

Stories
Behind
the Story

The events I'm about to cover take us back more than twenty years—this was before microprocessors, before hand-held calculators, before pacemakers, before man even walked on the moon. In order to help establish some sort of time perspective with reference to the overall history of electronic musical instrument design, let me point out that twenty-plus years ago, during the 1960s, I had marked my 25th year in the electronic organ field. Also, in a different setting, some innovative newcomers—who are now famous "old-timers"—had just arrived on the musical scene. Don Buchla, Bob Moog, and Wendy Carlos began experimenting with voltage-controlled, analog oscillators and amplifiers. Carlos' "Switched-On-Bach" was first heard in public in 1968, and stunned the audience. The work of musical innovators, such as these three, led to an instrument which instantly captured a great deal of popular attention, the "synthesizer." Allen was not involved in these developments, except perhaps in some peripheral way. For example, I recall that Bob Moog and I talked about a partnership of some sort, but nothing came of it. Allen Organ was into something quite different.

Today many people know about synthesizers, about "Switched-On-Bach," and about the stories behind them. Only a few people know about what Allen Organ was up to back then and the impact we had on the world of electronic musical instrument design. Even fewer people know about the intrigues beneath the surface—the stories behind the story. In view of this, I hope to present some detailed commentary about these stories, as best I can, on the pages that follow. The material is dedicated not only to those interested in understanding the technical history of electronic musical instruments but it is also aimed at those who want to dig beneath the surface and draw their own conclusions about broader, additional issues based on these newly presented facts and opinions. Before I begin, let me just add that this part of the history of the Allen Organ Company was, for me personally, both heaven and hell. I was privileged to rub shoulders with some of the finest of people, and I painfully learned a lot about the other kind.

Looking back on the broad scene at that time, I believe it's worth noting that the "Watergate" tragicomedy was still being "acted out" behind the scenes. Most of us were still woefully naive about such things as "dirty tricks," "covert operations," "stone-walling," etc. As for me, I was basically an old-fashioned, self-taught business man. By this time in my life, I knew the world wasn't lily white; however, I was used to dealing with people who were basically decent. In my world, at that time, there was an unwritten code of ethics among those with whom I dealt. We all knew that the code was sometimes stretched a bit, but it was just taken for granted that the code would certainly never be broken. It was like a sandlot baseball game. You expected some rough play, but you never had to worry about cyanide in your soda pop. At least that's the way it was in Allentown.

Entering
the Brave
New World

On October 30, 1968, I received a telephone call from a man named Ralph Deutsch. Ralph Deutsch was employed in a scientific capacity in Anaheim, California, for what was then known as the Autonetics Division of North American Rockwell Corporation. One of his jobs also appeared to involve establishing commercial markets for Autonetic's new MOS/LSI (Metal-Oxide Semiconductor/Large-Scale Integrated) circuit technology. This exotic technology was developed for military and space applications, but Autonetics now wanted to capitalize on the new technology by selling custom-designed MOS/LSI circuit devices to companies in the commercial sector.

The message on the telephone was absolutely captivating, even though some of the language was completely foreign to me—what I might now call "Anaheim tech-speak." However, one thing came through loud and clear. Deutsch and Rockwell were developing a new musical system based on technologies totally unfamiliar to me. They wanted to establish a joint venture with a musical instrument manufacturer such as Allen Organ Company in order to create a commercial market for their radically new technology. They had built something admittedly primitive to demonstrate their ideas and Deutsch invited either me or someone I would designate to come to Anaheim and listen to a demonstration.

Frankly, I was flattered by a call from such a giant corporation. By comparison, Allen Organ was miniscule in size. I couldn't believe that Rockwell, so famous for its connection with the fabulous Apollo moon flight mission, would be approaching "little" Allen Organ with a joint-venture proposal.

I told Deutsch that I would get back to him soon and promptly called our Los Angeles dealer to ask whether someone from there could check out this new musical system to see if it was "for real." Ron Schag and James Corcoran, the two principals of the dealership, agreed to make a preliminary investigation and report their findings to me. I called Deutsch to let him know that soon he should expect to hear from our representatives in Los Angeles about their visiting him and getting a demonstration. This indeed occurred within a day or so at the Rockwell facility in Anaheim. Ron Schag promptly got back to me with his findings. He said that Deutsch had showed them an experimental device which he used in the demonstration. Schag was sufficiently impressed with what he saw that he recommended that I personally take a look. Based on this advice, I wrote Deutsch indicating that I was prepared to go to California.

After further communication with Deutsch expressing Allen's interest, plans were made for me to visit Rockwell in mid-November. We arranged an appointment to meet at Rockwell's corporate offices near the Los Angeles' airport. So, on the designated day, I made my way to the headquarters of Rockwell, not knowing just what to expect.

As I approached the office building, I was awestruck. I had never dealt with such a massive organization before. There were so many people, some in military uniforms. I was duly impressed even before entering the multi-story office structure. After checking in through the security system, I met the man who called me on the phone a few weeks earlier, Ralph Deutsch. Others were also there including Harold Downes, a Vice President. When the cordialities were completed, we entered the elevator, which was to convey us to the roof. Another wave of awe shot through me. There, on a pad, was a helicopter ready to whisk us to the Anaheim facility many miles away. Although I had never been in a helicopter before, I never batted an eye upon entering. The President of Allen Organ Company of Macungie, Pennsylvania, appeared calm, cool, and collected—as though riding helicopters was part of my daily routine. However, my heart had a mind of its own, and it was revving up along with the chopper blades.

Arriving at Anaheim, we landed on another roof. As we descended into the building, I tried to focus my mind on the business at hand—an objective assessment of what all this might mean to Allen Organ. We entered the room containing the new system, and I saw it for the first time face to face.

I immediately recognized a Lowery spinet organ console, but coming out of it was a cable which was hooked into a strange looking piece of equipment. Deutsch took over the conversation and discussed the unit, explaining that this was a purely experimental system that was built to demonstrate some of the potential of their newly evolving ideas regarding the design and construction of organs. He further explained that with a development effort based on the wonders of space-age microelectronics, the whole tone generator of an organ with total harmonic control could be shrunk to the size of a magazine.

Mr. Downes had touched on the joint-venture plan. Allen would fund the project and provide the organ/musical know-how. Rockwell would do the engineering design, manufacture the resulting MOS/LSI circuit devices, and provide technical support. Allen would have exclusive rights to the new digital organ technology, would buy the MOS/LSI circuit devices from Rockwell, and assemble and sell organs based on the new technology.

I must have expressed some incredulity when listening to the primitive sounds of the experimental system because both Deutsch and Mr. Downes essentially said not to worry because Rockwell was well on its way to putting a man on the moon. Having this obvious expertise, they could guarantee that any problems I had with sound quality could be solved.

I had been presented with a myriad of factors to consider. The picture Rockwell painted was spellbinding. However, the stakes were enormous. Allen's future as a company was on the line. I had both positive and negative feelings about the situation. Let me share some of my thoughts from that point in time.

On the plus side, I was very impressed with Deutsch's description of the harmonic-control capabilities of the proposed tone generator. The harmonics available to create a sound are somewhat analogous to the colors available to create a painting. He said that I would have precise control over the 24 harmonics generated by the system at that time. To me, this was a most exciting prospect. I had been using a spectrum analyzer in my work with analog tone generators and knew about the sounds of tones in relation to their harmonic structures. The problem with the analog generators was that the harmonic structures could not be controlled at will. It was a frustrating hit-or-miss proposition. So, Deutsch's portrayal of the new system's total harmonic control made a great, positive impression on me.

It was obvious to me that Deutsch played a central role in the technicalities of the new system. He did all the talking, at least with regard to the technicalities. During my visit he readily "volunteered" that he was the inventor of the digital organ concept and was its program manager at Rockwell. Among other things, he had taught electronics and had authored scientific books, one of which was even translated into Russian. I was duly impressed with such heavy academic and scientific credentials.

What I "saw" at Rockwell was definitely impressive. I "saw" the radically new technology associated with the space program. I "saw" the microchips which apparently had been used by the military for some time but were just now being made available to the commercial world. I "saw" the promise of incredible size and cost reduction made possible by the use of space-age electronics, not to mention the increase in reliability. I could visualize all kinds of organ-design possibilities given a small, low-cost, high-quality, highly-reliable tone generator.

On the minus side, I knew that the sounds I actually "heard" were definitely not very impressive. In fact, in no way did the sounds I "heard" compare favorably with the electronic organs prevalent on the market at that time—including the Allen, of course. On the other hand, I had been assured by the Rockwell people that if

Allen entered into a development program with them, the results would be stupendous.

Of course, there were a lot of other less tangible factors with which to deal. The feeling of flattery I experienced upon receiving that first call from Rockwell had been diluted. I had first naively assumed that Allen was the first company "selected" by Rockwell to be honored by the joint venture proposal. During my visit, I learned that Rockwell had already approached other companies in the organ field. In fact, although I didn't know it at the time, I ultimately found out that Allen was actually the last to be called! At any rate, what I was told then was that although Rockwell was in contact with other companies, they definitely wanted to do business with Allen—assuming I didn't keep them waiting too long for an answer. Naturally, I responded with concern under the threat that if we didn't act quickly this new opportunity might be grabbed up by a competitor with resultant dire consequences for Allen.

With a mixed but heavy bag of ponderables, I returned to Allentown. After discussing the whole thing with my executive associates, we decided to take the gamble. In the following months, more visits were made in both directions to work out the details of the joint venture. Attorneys on both sides wrestled with the contracts. We on the Allen side did our best to ensure that the technical specifications were correct; however, we sure were inept in our comprehension of the new technology. I don't fault us, however. We were wrestling with a brand-new technology and, by definition, this meant that not many people understood it at that time. At any rate, when we got to the technical details of the contracts, we expressed our requirements in the technical language familiar to us and Deutsch "translated" these requirements into the "foreign" language of the new technology. We didn't understand the "foreign" language of the new technology; however, we had no reason to be concerned with this procedure because, after all, we felt that we were in a "joint venture." Rockwell and Allen would be partners. Obviously, in a joint venture, in order for each company to succeed individually, both companies have to work towards the success of the combined enterprise. In other words, there seemed to be a spirit of harmony and mutual cooperation at that time.

Negotiations concluded in May, 1969, with several agreements including the license, the patent, and the development contracts whereby Allen would pay Rockwell substantial monies and royalties should the development meet our expectations. Patents which would result from the program would be exclusively licensed to Allen. Allen would be obligated to convey cash and securities in the amount of at least one and one-half million dollars to Rockwell.

The
Development
of the
Digital Organ

The agreements signed in May of 1969 covered
many complex aspects of the joint venture between the
two companies, Allen Organ and Rockwell. The details
would probably make an excellent case study for law
students, but the actual specifics of the documents are
beyond the scope of this text. However, it's easy to
understand the general idea behind the joint venture.
The common element between the two companies was
the "digital organ," something that only existed in the
roughest concept in early 1969. The "digital" part was
Rockwell's forte. The "organ" part was to be Allen's. It
was a classic synergism. Neither company acting alone
could create the world's first, commercially-viable,
digital musical instrument, but both companies acting
cooperatively had a good chance of succeeding.

Although a team of engineers had been assembled
at Rockwell to work on the project, all technical matters

were handled through Ralph Deutsch. I knew that Deutsch wanted to guarantee himself a role in the project. In fact, he had asked me privately to request a clause in the agreements requiring Rockwell to keep him prominently on the project. Such a clause was indeed added to the agreements. On the surface it seemed harmless, even to our advantage, to have Deutsch continue on as a central figure in the project. At that time, I thought of Deutsch as a scientist who, quite understandably, wanted to be a part of what promised to be a remarkable technical achievement.

To be perfectly frank, I was still somewhat in awe of Ralph Deutsch. I might compare my dealing with Deutsch to dealing with a highly skilled surgeon. The surgeon is privy to knowledge beyond most people's comprehension; therefore, I believe it's fair to say most people would be somewhat in awe of such a surgeon— especially if such a surgeon were prone to "explain" things using the specialized language of medicine. I believe it's also fair to say that most people would reasonably place their trust in such a specialist rather than try to become personally proficient in the specialty. Such was the case at that time with my dealings with Ralph Deutsch.

I was told by Deutsch that various engineers at Rockwell had already been working on the digital organ project before the agreements were signed, but it wasn't until after the official signing that I was able to get a first-hand feel for the actual "modus operandi" back in

Anaheim. Although Deutsch was always in the limelight, I noticed that he often had to consult another engineer, Dr. George Watson, when it came to certain details. In my opinion, Dr. Watson was the antithesis of Deutsch in personality. Although both men were highly-trained specialists, Watson was always the quintessence of tasteful modesty who worked diligently in the background while Deutsch, having no "handicap" of humility, honed a fine skill at dashing to the foreground. I'll have more to say in a following chapter about George Watson, an unsung hero of modern electronic musical instrument design. Additional Rockwell engineers who were visible to me were Glen Griffith and Sam Muryama.

The digital organ project was divided into two stages. The first stage was the development of an engineering model which was used to "prove out," in actual hardware, the many new concepts which had to be devised to make the digital organ a practical reality. The engineering model was built using standard digital parts. The ultimate goal, of course, was to create a commercially-viable, digital organ using Rockwell's custom-designed, MOS/LSI (Metal-Oxide Semiconductor/Large-Scale Integrated) circuit devices. This was to be the second stage of the project—the designing and building of the actual production prototype of the digital organ.

In accordance with the contracts, we shipped Rockwell two stripped down organs including console,

Front view of engineering development model of the digital organ.

keys, stops, and audio system. The Rockwell engineers labored through the summer breaking new ground in developing a brand-new electronic organ design methodology and incorporating it into the engineering model. From my vantage point, things seemed to be going well with the joint venture. I recall visiting California with my wife and son, Steven, in July of 1969, with a stop in Anaheim. Our treatment by everyone at Rockwell was most gracious. We were even invited to Deutsch's home in Sherman Oaks, and had a pleasant visit.

Work steadily continued on the engineering model until finally, in September, 1969, I received a call from Deutsch proclaiming triumph. He said that they had solved the last design problem and after they did some minor cleanup work the engineering model would be ready for me to check out the following month. So, in October, I was again off to California, very excited about the prospect of reaching this critical milestone.

Upon arrival in Anaheim, I began to study the ins and outs of this brand-new machine—the engineering model of the digital organ. I had to go mainly on instinct because I certainly didn't understand this new technology. All my experience was in analog electronics; now here I was facing a radically different digital world. My viewpoint was from the old school with rules I understood, but the new technology had its own set of rules which I had to explore before I could understand. It was like being dropped into a strange, foreign country with unfamiliar customs. Does a head shaking up and down mean "yes" or does it perhaps mean "no"? Even in this kind of situation, I believe it was reasonable to expect that a trustful give-and-take process would take place between the individuals of each culture until a mutual understanding was reached.

To me, the engineering model was the vehicle for fostering such a trustful give-and-take process between the Anaheim and Macungie people. To me, it was self-evident that the engineering model was not the final goal. It was a research and exploratory vehicle—a vehicle for learning—and a means to the ultimate goal of manufacturing better organs. This is how I approached the engineering model and that particular visit to Anaheim. I might add that after a year of working with Deutsch I hadn't the slightest reason to believe that he didn't feel the same way about the need for trustful give-and-take.

Deutsch went over the essential aspects of the engineering model for me. He showed me the alterable-voice card reader which was provided to facilitate my evaluation and selection of voices for the production prototype. The card reader was a quick way to load a trial waveshape (tone) into the waveshape memory of the engineering model and listen to it. After a waveshape was accepted, the pattern on the card was to be transferred into a pattern of diodes on a diode-matrix board which served as the waveshape memory. Remember, this was long before EPROMs

(Erasable Programmable Read Only Memories)—those amazing little devices that are so familiar to computer buffs in today's world.

Our conversation eventually turned to the production prototype—the hardware that we would actually be using to build production organs. At that point Deutsch dropped the bomb! He "informed" me that the expression system in the production prototype would have to be modified from the one specified in the contracts. I told him that, from an organ designer's point of view, the proposed modification would result in a major deficiency in the organ. Deutsch protested that it was no big deal. I was taken aback at Deutsch's brusque dismissal of my genuine concern. I felt that this was an "organ" matter, clearly an issue best judged by the "organ" half of the partnership, Allen Organ Company. Swallowing my pride a bit, I suggested that we should get someone from Allen other than me to judge the situation from the organist's point of view. Deutsch agreed. I called Dayton Johnson, my assistant, back in Allentown and requested that he come out to California on short notice to help resolve an important issue. He assured me that he'd be there the following day—a Saturday as I recall—and did, in fact, arrive on the scene the next day.

After listening to Deutsch's description of the new expression arrangement, Dayton was as horrified as I expected. The new arrangement eliminated the separate expression of the Swell division of the organ as was specified in the contracts. As any church organist knows, the Swell division is supposed to be separately expressed. In fact, the word "Swell" is used to name the division because the organist is supposed to be able to separately make that division "swell" or enlarge in sound amplitude by depressing a pedal called the "Swell expression pedal." Eliminating this feature was certainly going to be a problem for us, a fact which Dayton eloquently explained to Deutsch.

Deutsch's response to this technical issue was as troubling to me as the issue itself. The cordial, accommodating, smooth-talking Deutsch seemed to dissolve before my eyes. I was now facing a Deutsch who appeared to me to be on the verge of nervous collapse. He acted as though he had been personally violated in some way.

I did not understand his behavior; it was disturbing to me. As I mentioned before, I was still somewhat in awe of Deutsch. Until now, the technical jargon had flowed ever so confidently from his mouth that I had been lulled into a sense of security about the eventual success of the project. Now he appeared to me as being rather emotionally distraught. Imagine that you are about to have surgery and you see that your surgeon has suddenly lost his composure. I believe your feelings in that situation would be similar to the feelings I experienced at that time as I watched Deutsch dissolve.

It was not until sixteen years later that I received some insight into the reason for Deutsch's puzzling behavior. In October, 1985, James Southard testified, in a litigation proceeding, as follows regarding Deutsch's visit to Southard's company, Conn, in September of 1968: "I think that he said something to the effect that if he didn't sell this thing, he may be walking the street, or something to that effect."

As I understand Southard's testimony, it meant that Deutsch's job was on the line depending on how financially successful the organ project would be for Rockwell. I didn't realize at the time how much pressure he must have been under. This would explain why I was initially treated so well by Deutsch. I didn't understand enough of the technology to create any waves for him, and he made every effort to keep it that way. When we finally encountered an issue which I did fully understand—the elimination of the separate Swell expression pedal—I made plenty of waves indeed. There was no possible way for Deutsch to "tech-talk" his way out of it. Judging from my recollection of his emotional behavior in dealing with the "expression" issue, Deutsch apparently feared that I would suddenly abandon the project or take 'some similar drastic step—creating a threat to his career. He knew that the other organ companies had rejected the joint-venture organ-project. In essence, he was stuck with Jerome Markowitz and facing a serious "organ" issue. We were now in my court and, I believe, he simply panicked. As for me, I only wanted to resolve the issue sensibly and get on with the project.

Fortunately, William Sauers, the Rockwell executive assigned to the joint venture at the time, took charge and ushered us into the privacy of his office. I took some time to gather my thoughts as Deutsch appeared to be on the verge of a breakdown.

I was fascinated by the card reader which Rockwell provided as a laboratory aid in coming up with voicing waveshapes to be stored in the final organ. What if we could offer a card reader as a sales feature on the final organ? It seemed to me that such a feature would definitely add to the viability of the organ in the marketplace. It would help to counteract the negatives we would face in the market with the "less-than-ideal" expression arrangement. So, with this in mind, I offered to back off on the expression issue if Rockwell would incorporate the card reader and some other minor items into the final organ. After some study, Rockwell agreed to my proposals—for a price.

Because of the additional circuit complexity, we would have to purchase two, additional MOS/LSI devices for the organs equipped with the card reader. I agreed to do this and left Anaheim having weathered the first storm.

By the end of the year, more voices were added to the engineering model and Dayton Johnson again went to Anaheim for more listening tests. At this point, he encountered one of those rules about the new digital technology which we didn't anticipate because of our "old school" analog perspective. This involved tuning

accuracy. Of course, we didn't comprehend the reason
for the out-of-tuneness then. All Dayton could say for
sure was that the engineering model had a tuning
problem. Obviously, something had to be done to
correct the problem.

I explained our problem to Deutsch, who was again
unsympathetic to our "organ" problem. In a letter to
me, dated January 9, 1970, Deutsch spelled out in cold,
calculated terms what he portrayed as "Rockwell's"
position on the matter. The gist of the letter, as I read
it, was something like this—tough luck, guys! Our
measurements prove that we met the "contractual
requirements with respect to frequency," and if you now
want something else, it's going to cost you! Have a nice
day.

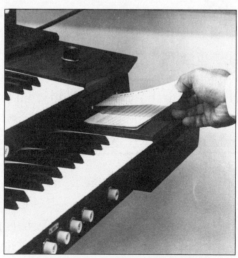

Demonstrating the operation of the
alterable voice card reader—1971.

He also made it clear that the engineering model would remain in Rockwell's possession until Allen came up with a "plan of action." It just so happened that I had been asking that we bring the engineering model to Allentown so I could get on with the voicing studies. It was important to me to get on with the voicing studies so we would be able to develop viable production models. So, Deutsch's withholding of the engineering model from us was especially irksome. His behavior when facing technical problems reminded me more of the playground than the business world.

We agreed to a price increase for the MOS/LSI devices in order to improve the frequency accuracy and I finally received the engineering model in Allentown for my voicing work. The voicing procedure consisted of punching harmonic amplitude data onto an IBM card and running a computer program which converted the harmonic data into a corresponding waveshape. The waveshape data was then punched onto another IBM card which, when inserted into the card reader of the engineering model, allowed me to play the waveshape as a stop on an organ. Recordings of pipes served as a guide in arranging the harmonics to create different voices. The variations seemed endless; I never had so much control over voicing.

Interestingly, we didn't have a computer to run the voicing program. However, General Acceptance Corporation in Allentown graciously allowed us to rent time on their IBM/360. In those days it took a day to turn around one voice test, but the excitement of exploring a brand-new technology took the edge off my impatience. I gradually homed in on an acceptable set of voices which we programmed onto the diode matrix boards in order to test the complete organ specification. This information was sent to Rockwell for entering into the MOS/LSI read-only memories to be used in the final MOS/LSI version of the digital organ.

Back in Anaheim, work continued on the design of thirteen custom MOS/LSI devices. The final MOS/LSI version of the digital organ, the production prototype, contained 22 of these devices, some being used in multiples. All 22 MOS/LSI devices were mounted on a single, printed-circuit board which formed the tone generator of the organ. The relatively small size and neat appearance of the "MOS Board" veiled the true complexity of the electronic circuitry lying within the MOS/LSI devices. About 48,000 transistors were contained on that single, tone-generator board—a phenomenal accomplishment in 1970.

Toward the end of 1970, the completion of the MOS/LSI production prototype organ was drawing near. The plan was for Rockwell to deliver two production prototypes to Allen for checkout and official acceptance. Everything was going fairly smoothly at this point and my thoughts were turning towards manufacturing and marketing concerns. These were major concerns, I might add, considering the revolutionary nature of the new technology and all the reorientation it would necessitate both in the Company and with our dealers. My planning had aimed the new technology at mid-sized organs, a realistically challenging goal in my view. In short, we would have our hands full but everything seemed to be in place. However, in November, Deutsch and two Rockwell executives came to Macungie with a whole new proposal. They wanted to expand our relationship to include the development of a "small organ." I wasn't very enthusiastic. The production prototypes relating to the contracts of May, 1969, were not even delivered for acceptance yet. Moreover, we had already incurred huge financial obligations in relation to those contracts. Accordingly, we were reluctant to commit to such an expansion of the project at that time.

Although all three of the men from Rockwell tried to sell me on the idea of expanding the project, Deutsch was, by far, the most adamant and aggressive in his tactics. He seemed quite frustrated that he couldn't force me to cave in and accept his new plan. I neither knew what was going on behind the scenes at that time nor did I know just how deeply my rejection of Deutsch's "small organ" proposal irritated him. Nor could I imagine how significantly the rejection would affect our future relationship. Events, which would occur much later, ultimately opened my eyes to many things that were hidden from my view in that time frame. These revelations, the "story behind the story," will be of interest not only to those involved with the electronic musical instrument industry but also to students of business in general. However, to maintain historical continuity, I'll go into that later.

Finally, towards the end of December, 1970, delivering the final pieces of the two production prototypes, Deutsch and two Rockwell engineers brought two, completed "MOS Boards" to Macungie. After a time, they had the boards working in one of the two organs we had prepared to receive the "MOS Boards." There were some last minute glitches, but the moment had come for us to formally accept that amazing product of so many man-years of effort, the world's first digital electronic musical instrument to be placed into production. By January 1971, I formally accepted the production prototypes, and turned over to Rockwell the money and Allen Organ securities representing the financial obligations as specified in the contracts of May, 1969. With this momentous event behind me, my thoughts quickly returned to manufacturing and marketing.

A complete set of circuit boards comprising the
entire digital tone generation system—1971.

George
Watson–
an Unsung
Hero

In 1967, Dr. George Watson, working for North American Rockwell now known as Rockwell International, was assigned to a project which would ultimately produce the world's first digital organ.

The effort leading to the project was managed by Ralph Deutsch and was probably initiated in response to an anticipated downturn in the aerospace business. Rockwell wanted to develop commercial markets for their space-age "MOS/LSI" circuit devices, and the electronic organ industry was one of their targets.

Looking back, Rockwell's proposals to somehow interject their exotic new technology into the then older, proven analog world of electronic organs was met with a lot of skepticism by most of the organ companies of that day. It was perceived as radical and financially questionable. Indeed, the success of the project would require an expensive and extraordinary effort—plus

94

conceptual breakthroughs. Fate brought George Watson to the scene. In retrospect, he was the right person in the right place at the right time to "pull it off."

Aside from his strong engineering background, Watson had some musical experience with a small, home-type electronic organ. He knew that using "MOS/LSI" technology to build an organ would require radically new approaches such as the intensive use of time-division multiplexing.

Rockwell engineers, George Watson standing
and Glen Griffith testing one of the original "MOS/LSI"
circuit boards at Rockwell—1970.

One of his most elegant insights was recognizing that an organist can hardly play more than twelve keys simultaneously. In other words, people rarely use more than ten fingers and two feet to press the keys. Therefore, twelve tone-generating entities are sufficient in the organ — as long as each of the twelve entities can "play" any of the keys of the instrument. He invented the concept of "note-generator assignment" to handle, in real time, the incredible coordination between rapidly changing key patterns and the "note-limited," general-purpose tone generators. Many other problems had to be solved and new techniques invented.

Watson's system was a brilliant technical achievement. In 1971, it was first incorporated into a commercial product known as the Allen Digital Computer Organ. The electronic musical instrument industry would never be the same. Many of the organ companies in existence in the 1970s steadfastly refused to accept the power of the new technology. However, by the early 1980s, the rush to adopt Watson's "note-limited system" was underway; today, virtually every synthesizer, electronic keyboard, electronic organ, and the like utilizes the invention described in George Watson's pioneering U.S. Patent 3,160,799.

In today's electronic ambiance—TV, radio, cassettes, compact discs, musical scoring of movies, etc., which all make extensive use of electronic keyboards— most people are actually listening to a reflection of

George Watson's genius. A spate of "historical" articles has appeared in recent years in electronic music publications with never a mention of George Watson. This is a sad commentary on the depth of knowledge of present-day commentators and writers in this field.

Patents
& Intellectual
Property

As far back as the fifteenth century, man has had to deal with the consequences of obtaining specialized knowledge. In those days, master craftsmen taught apprentices a craft—this was good for both master and apprentice. The apprentice learned the craft; the master profited from the apprentice's low-cost labor. After an apprentice learned the craft from the master, he was not supposed to take advantage of the master by using the newly gained knowledge to hurt the master's business. Needless to say, not everyone played by these rules and problems arose. Courts entered into the picture and tried to determine what was fair. Eventually, the concept of legal protection of intellectual property evolved.

Realization that a modern society thrives on technological innovation has long been recognized. The invention of new or improved processes, machines, and manufactured products is good for society if the inventor discloses his discoveries to the public. This is how technological progress builds on itself. By disclosing the invention, the inventor gives everyone a head start in working on the next invention rather than having to reinvent what has already been discovered. However, to be fair, the inventor should get some reward for his contribution to society. Today, we have the concept of the "patent," patent laws, and a special government agency, the "Patent Office," set up not only to foster the dissemination of newly obtained knowledge but also to protect the owners of resulting intellectual property via the issuance of patents.

In order to receive a patent, an inventor must fully disclose his discovery to the public. In return, he is granted an exclusive right to the use of the invention for a set period of time—seventeen years in the U.S.A. This gives the inventor the right to use the courts to prevent others from using the invention—"infringing" on the invention. By this mechanism, the inventor is supposed to be able to profit fairly from his efforts before others unfairly take advantage of his sharing the knowledge about his discoveries.

The above explanation of how the patent system works is ultra-simplistic. In reality, the situation is much more complex. For example, the granting of a patent by the Patent Office can be subsequently rescinded by the court. Because of this fact and the penchant for litigation in this country, many patent matters end up in court. Unfortunately, the court may not be the best place to settle patent matters fairly. Patents deal with highly-complex technical issues which neither judges nor juries are readily able to fathom. Therefore, the judgment of patent issues by courts is wide open to manipulation by unscrupulous lawyers and witnesses.

A patent grant may be considered to be a covenant between the government (representing the public) and the inventor who, in essence, receives a "protected territory" for seventeen years. In the past, cases existed where inventors artificially tried to extend the seventeen-year monopoly period by not applying for the patent in a timely fashion. For example, if an inventor began producing and selling the product for a significant period of time before applying for the patent, he could piggyback the time during which the product was being produced and sold over and above the seventeen years from the date of the patent grant. Subsequently, the law was changed in order to limit this seventeen-year period. Now, an inventor applying for a patent must execute an oath in which, among other things, the inventor swears that the new device has neither been on sale, nor been in public use, nor been publicly disclosed prior to one year before the date of the patent application. Anyone involved with patents soon learns that this is a sacred rule which must not be broken; the penalty for breaking this rule, if detected, is invalidation of the patent by the courts.

Another factor involving patents had to be worked out over the years. Today, most technological development is funded by institutions or companies. Inventions are still conceived in the minds of real human beings. Therefore, recognizing this, the United States Patent Office only grants patents to human beings. As a result, institutions and companies cannot be named as an inventor on a patent.

In consideration for the financial backing provided by the institutions and companies in supporting the process of technological advancement, the law provides for the assignment of the rights to a patent to the supporting institution or company. Thus, scientists and engineers are hired and remunerated for inventing (and receiving patents in their own name) on behalf of their employer. In return, they sign an agreement assigning the rights to their inventions to their employer while they are employed and for some reasonable time, usually one year, after they terminate their employment. The simple idea behind this is that the employer is entitled to capitalize on the new technology funded by the institution or company. This process is supposed to establish the rules in a fair manner. For example, it would hardly be fair for an inventor to develop an idea on company time, to use company resources, and then to terminate his employment and file for a patent on the idea, thus leaving the company with nothing.

How this all relates to the story of the digital organ is reflected in chapters which follow.

Honoring the Intellectual Property of Others

Until 1964, like most other manufacturers of keyboard instruments, Allen Organ Company purchased complete keyboards from a supplier who specialized in the production and supply of such items. These were considered difficult to manufacture. In fact, up to that time, Allen had purchased thousands of these keyboards mainly from Pratt Reed & Company, located in Ivoryton, Connecticut.

I suppose there was a connection between the name of the town and the Pratt Reed keyboard operation because for many years, before conservationists called the world's attention to the possible extinction of elephants, most keyboards of pianos and organs consisted of wooden sticks divided into white "naturals" and black "sharps" with the naturals covered with ivory.

We considered the keyboards to be a relatively expensive component in our products; therefore, during

1964, we applied considerable effort to the thought of manufacturing keyboards "in-house." Over the years, aside from the cost problem, we had grown uncomfortable with the "one-of-a-kind" nature of the keyboards manufactured in those days. This quirk of the keyboards was due to the method of manufacture. All the keys of a particular keyboard, which for an organ consists of a set of 61 wooden keysticks, were cut from a single slab of wood in many passes through a bandsaw. No two keyboards were cut identically. Often, a given key of one keyboard was not interchangeable with the corresponding key of another keyboard. This led to some problems at our end relating to the replacement of individual, defective keys. For example, there was occasional spoilage of keys during our manufacturing processes. Also, occasionally an owner of one of our instruments would suffer damage to a given key or keys and would approach us for a replacement. The hand-tailoring of a replacement key to make it fit into an existing keyboard was a real problem.

Finally, in 1964, we came up with an idea for a new type of keyboard in which the wooden part of each key was identical to the wooden part of every other key. Let me elaborate.

A keyboard is divided into octaves of twelve keys each. If we look closely at the front part of a keyboard, we see that the pattern of key shapes repeats for each octave. Also, there are only seven, different, white-key shapes; all the black keys have the same shape. Our idea was to use molded plastic "caps" to create the front part of each key. Only seven different shapes in white caps and one shape in black caps were needed. Before the caps were installed, all the short wooden keysticks looked identical in shape and spacing. Attaching the appropriate cap to each keystick gave each key its required shape, color, and feel from the viewpoint of the performer. Manufacturing cost was reduced; replacement of individual defective keys became trivial. Eureka! As the idea evolved, we became enthused enough to buy expensive plastic injection molds from an injection molding company for the mass production of the key caps.

As the project proceeded, I became even more excited as I realized that we had probably come upon a patentable idea. We instructed our patent attorneys to make a "search." This is a procedure involving the examination of all previous inventions to make sure that we had not been preempted by an earlier inventor. Well, lo and behold, we found that we had indeed reinvented the wheel! In fact, the inventor turned out to be an employee of Pratt Reed Company, with the patent assigned to that company. Obviously, we now had no chance to patent the idea. Yet, having already committed a substantial investment to our project, we were reluctant to abandon it.

I communicated with Stan Renehan, our sales contact with Pratt Reed, and he invited me to come up to their plant for a discussion. This occurred toward the end of 1964. I found Pratt Reed was quite reasonable about the matter and suggested that we pay them a royalty on each key that we would manufacture in return for which they would license us to freely produce these keys for our products. The cost of manufacturing each key, including the royalty that we were to pay Pratt Reed, would amount to substantially less than what we were previously paying them. It seemed like an excellent solution.

So, on January 1, 1965, our licensing agreement with Pratt Reed went into effect; during that year, for the first time, we began producing our own keyboards. The original royalty arrangement remained in effect until 1976. The patent was not due to expire until 1981. However, during 1976, we suggested to Pratt Reed that we pay them a single, final lump sum so that we could discard the record keeping that was involved in submitting royalty reports and the like. They agreed.

During 1974, we had a somewhat similar experience. One of our employees came up with the idea of producing a new kind of tremolo unit. This unit would provide an effect that was quite desirable when used in conjunction with our instruments, as well as those of other manufacturers. Again, we thought we had a patentable idea and ordered our patent attorneys to make a search. Once again we were faced with the same situation. An employee of a subsidiary of CBS—

CBS had begun to acquire musical instrument manufacturers—beat us to the punch.

By the time we became fully aware of the existence of a patent situation, we had already committed resources to manufacturing the device. In 1975, I was able to work out a license with CBS. Once again we were in a position to produce a device that we needed. Even though we had to pay a royalty to the owner of the patent, the total cost was still more economical than any other method.

At least based upon these two experiences, it is clear that patent problems between companies can be solved by licensing agreements that are mutually advantageous. On the other hand, had Pratt Reed or CBS made outrageous demands upon us, or had they simply refused to let us use their patents, or had we ignored their intellectual property rights, we would have been faced with a far different set of problems. The lesson I learned was that a reasonable royalty demand by a patent owner can help to avoid the unpleasantries and expense of litigation. The other essential ingredient to avoiding litigation is a patent user who honors the intellectual property of others. Later on, I applied this lesson to patents which we owned and wanted to license. I always sought simple, business-like agreements. However, my strategy only worked if the other party was also seeking a simple, business-like agreement— one honoring our intellectual property.

Ralph Deutsch & the Dark Side

With the digital organ designed and the prototype from Rockwell officially approved by Allen in January of 1971, we are at a point in the story of the digital organ where we were supposed to "live happily ever after." Well, this idyllic ending never materialized; life turned out to be much more complicated than expected. There is what I call the dark side of the story about the digital organ and its aftermath. This dark side doesn't in any way detract from the fact that the development of the digital organ was an extraordinary technical achievement as well as a business success.

It is important to know that details of this dark side came to light only after many years of legal proceedings. Most of the information upon which this part of the story is based came forth as a by-product of several litigations into which we were forced after the digital organ was developed. I'll talk about these litigations in other chapters. With the benefit of twenty additional years of experience and the information subsequently uncovered, I'm now in a much more knowledgeable position to talk about the "behind the scenes" aspects of the digital organ story. When the events were actually taking place, either I was deliberately kept in the dark or I was just too naive to put two and two together. I shall summarize the main points of this dark side story, at least as much of it as I've been able to piece together so far. Later, I shall go into a little more detail.

Ralph Deutsch, until he came up with the digital organ idea, appeared to be one of countless technical people typically employed by a large, high-tech corporation. In the mid-1960s, well into his career, he had neither established any individual claim to fame among his peers, nor did he win any points as a team player. In fact, he had a reputation for being "difficult" and exhibiting childish behavior in his contacts with co-workers. As I see it, fate presented him with a unique opportunity to rise from obscurity—the digital organ idea. Because Rockwell, his employer, was receptive to ideas such as this at the time, it seems to me that he realized that if he played his cards right he could achieve personal "success" via the digital organ. I have no problem with this part. However, I was to be greatly troubled by the traits Deutsch exhibited in trying to achieve his "success." Later events would convince me that these traits suggested vindictiveness, mendacity, and Machiavellianism. Even more troubling was the apparent ease with which such an individual could manipulate people and institutions—including our legal system.

After Deutsch sold the digital organ idea to his management, he then had to get someone to engineer it and someone to pay for it because he was apparently much better at theory and hyperbole than he was at the practical and factual. Excellent engineers were already available from the winding down of the space program—including George Watson whom I mentioned in another chapter. Money to pay for Deutsch's idea had to come from the outside—from an organ manufacturer. Deutsch approached most of the leading organ manufacturers except Allen; they all refused to undertake the development project. In desperation and under pressure from his management, he finally approached Allen and got his funding. Apparently, he was reluctant to deal with Allen.

Being "stuck" with Allen as a partner was probably very frustrating for Deutsch. I was an "active" partner who had the audacity to stand up to Deutsch's intense protestations when serious "organ" issues arose. Unknown to me at the time, Deutsch presented to his management his own plan for Allen Organ which exaggerated the projected sales of digital organs. Although I had no knowledge of his "plan," he portrayed it to his management as "the" plan. As my own plan for the "Allen" digital organ was not congruent with his, I was obviously a thorn in his side.

I was tolerated out of necessity until I approved the prototype and turned over the development funds to Rockwell. At this point, beginning in the spring of 1971, Deutsch's interest in Allen Organ waned as his attention turned to the awakening giant overseas—Japan.

Allen had paid for and, therefore, legally controlled the use of the digital organ technology. By contract, Allen had a right of first refusal on subsequent digital music developments at Rockwell. As president of Allen, it was incumbent on me to rigorously protect Allen's rights to the new technology and exercise good judgment in controlling how it should be used. Deutsch's plans revolved around Japan; mine did not. Therefore, I did not go along with Deutsch's ideas. This must have been terribly frustrating to him in his self-appointed role as "Mr. Digital Organ." How could Deutsch exploit the digital organ technology for his own self-interest with Allen standing in the way? I hope that this question will be at least partially answered in the pages that follow.

Bringing the Digital Organ to Market

When the digital organ project was first described to me by Ralph Deutsch in late 1968, I had an erroneous impression. I thought after the design was completed and the MOS/LSI devices started to roll off Rockwell's production line, all we would have to do at Allen was connect them together per Rockwell's instructions. Obviously, I had an overly simplistic view of what it would be like to actually work with this new technology in our factory. I really believed that any problems related to the new technology would be handled by Rockwell; the rest we could handle ourselves. As Rockwell worked to get the prototypes together toward the end of 1970, I became more wary of the problems we might encounter getting the new technology into production.

Realizing that we had no one in our organization who really understood digital electronics, we decided to "beef up" our own, in-house, technical capability by hiring engineers with digital backgrounds. By mid-1971, we were successful in finding three engineers with the appropriate technical backgrounds who also were interested in working in the brand-new field of digital electronic musical instrument engineering. And there was plenty for them to do. We encountered a host of technical problems when we began to redirect some of our production operations toward building a few, selected organ models based on the new digital technology. I soon realized that getting daily help from Rockwell—3,000 miles away—was not practical. So, our three digital engineers were immediately pressed into service as they came aboard and received considerable "on-the-job" training.

I also braced myself for the impact the change-over would have on the general morale in our factory. For example, I was concerned about the feelings of our employees, many of whose jobs would be radically changed by the new technology. A large number of the skills which were diligently developed and proudly practiced by our employees over many years in an "analog" world simply did not apply to the new "digital" world. For example, the analog oscillator organs were built like the early televisions. Hundreds of electronic components had to be wired together individually. In contrast, the new digital organ was built like a modern computer. A relatively small number of micro-miniature, digital devices, each containing more than a thousand transistors, had to be mounted and soldered to high-precision, printed circuit boards. In other areas of specialization, such as tuning and voicing, jobs were also going to be dramatically affected. The analog oscillator organs required a substantial amount of manual tuning and voicing. With the new digital organ, the tuning and much of the voicing was controlled with such accuracy that very few manual adjustments were needed. In retrospect, considering the magnitude of the task, the transition from the old, analog-oriented job structure to the new, digital-oriented job structure was handled extremely well by all the people affected by the change-over. As

Allen Digital Engineer, Robert Woron, testing an Allen-built version of the Rockwell-designed digital tone generation system—early 1970s.

the new production methods were gradually put into place, our people were reassigned to learn the new skills required.

Because of all the obvious start-up problems we were going to face as well as the potential for many unforeseen problems associated with getting the new technology into production, I had decided to limit the introduction of the digital organ to just a few models in the middle of our model lineup. Some of these models were designed around one Rockwell system as originally planned; some other models were actually designed using two of the Rockwell systems. At some point along the way, I had thought of using more than one system in an organ in a kind of building block fashion. The idea proved to be quite effective.

We began building organs using two systems by simply using two separate sets of key contacts—one for each system. My ultimate plan was to extend this building block idea beyond two systems; however, at first we didn't have the means to key more than two systems in one organ. So, as we approached the official public unveilings of the new technology in the summer of 1971, we had a small lineup of models—the largest using two systems.

At this point, I should mention that the "newness" of the technology presented us with another problem— what to call the product. During the development, the term "digital organ" was generally used to describe the project. Of course, scientists and engineers knew what the term "digital" meant and could readily understand the significance of the term "digital organ." However, I knew I could not expect the same understanding of technical terminology from laymen. In reviewing all the technical names that could be applied to the new instruments, I finally chose the term "computer organ." I reasoned that most people had at least heard the term "computer" and knew it had something to do with accurate and fast mathematical calculations. In short, I knew the term "computer organ" was an apt, readily-understood description of our new product—a system which produced musical tones by performing torrents of mathematical computations on numbers at blazing speed.

On May 20, 1971, the "Allen Computer Organ" was revealed to the press at a press party hosted by Rockwell at the Hotel Waldorf Astoria in New York City. Although the actual public showing didn't occur until June, the press party certainly generated substantial positive publicity. Our product was correctly characterized as a "major industry breakthrough."

Finally, in June, the new instruments were put on display to the trade at the National Association of Music Merchants (NAMM) Show in Chicago. Our dealers had been given a private showing the day before. The reaction is well summarized by the following excerpted comments about the show from *ERA*, a music-trades publication of that time.

ORGANS

Allen's computerized church organ, which will soon become a LINE of several models, amounts to a technological "breakthrough". The product simply defies evaluation! There can be little doubt but that this new concept will enable Allen to completely dominate the church organ business in the early future. In a nutshell, this product will enable an ordinary church organist to almost approach "artist" capability. The product was a devastating success!

Indeed, the Allen Computer Organ sent waves through the electronic musical instrument industry. It also set precedent in a more general way. It shared the limelight, in 1971, with the Sharp calculator as being the world's first, digital-based consumer product offered for sale. I must admit I enjoyed all the fanfare, but I knew what counted most was how our dealers and customers felt about the new development. Therefore, I was especially happy about our booking a record number of orders at the NAMM Show of 1971.

The effect of our success on our competitors was predictable. Most of them were expecting the arrival of a digital organ product from Allen. Keep in mind that they were offered the concept by Rockwell, and they all declined. They didn't know exactly what to expect, but obviously they would not want the new technology to succeed. In view of the tremendous acceptance we did actually enjoy, several competitors quite ruthlessly "bad mouthed" the Computer Organ in hopes of frightening customers away. This touches on some of the more unsavory aspects of our industry which I'm saving for another chapter. So, suffice it to say here that the efforts to defame the Computer Organ were rather disturbing; but, in the end, the truth and overwhelming superiority of the new digital technology prevailed.

The distinction of being the very first customer to buy an Allen Computer Organ has to go to St. Mark's Evangelical Lutheran Church in Easton, Pennsylvania. We "quietly" sold that one during the spring of '71 in order to get some field experience and customer response as soon as possible. The response was excellent.

During the following year, sales of the new product accelerated, and in September, 1972, the Allen Digital Computer Organ was given an award by *Industrial Research* magazine as being one of the best one hundred new products of that year. This was the first time a musical instrument was honored by such an award.

The
Japanese
Connection

Today Japan is the preeminent force in the electronics industry including the electronic musical instrument business. Most of the prominent American companies in the field have either gone out of business or are now owned by the Japanese. The situation wasn't always so.

Back in the 1960s, the Japanese competed with many American companies in the electronic musical instrument business. The popular product then was the home organ; the technology used to design the organs was "analog." The digital organ, based on digital technology, was being developed behind closed doors in America by two American companies, North American Rockwell and Allen Organ Company.

Because the digital organ was such a revolutionary development in the art of electronic musical instrument design, the knowledge obtained by those working on the project was extremely valuable. As I indicated in an earlier chapter, situations involving valuable knowledge such as this led to the concept of intellectual property which, in turn, led to the laws governing such property. Obviously, one rule of good business management is to protect the valuable resources of the company rigorously, including intellectual property. Therefore, during the development of the digital organ, the knowledge obtained about how to actually build a practical digital organ was kept strictly confidential (as far as I know).

Of course, patents can be applied for and eventually may be issued. However, even after patents are issued, the owner of the related intellectual property must still rigorously defend against the ever-present, high-tech pirates. Three things which stack the cards in favor of the brigands are: the great cost of litigation, the difficulty of our courts to comprehend high-tech matters, and the great economic advantage of simply copying new developments after the development expense is paid for by someone else.

Another hazard faced by the owner of high-tech intellectual property is the temptation on the part of insiders to "sell out" to competitors for personal profit. When an insider sells "official," high-tech, national, secret information to another country and thereby jeopardizes the security of his own country, it is called treason. Furthermore, most people loathe the one who sells out. There is even a certain sensationalism associated with the story. When the same thing is done in the commercial world, most people are unconcerned. Thus, faced with these obstacles, the business manager trying to protect the intellectual property of his company has his work cut out for him.

Getting back to the development of the digital organ, the original contracts between Rockwell and Allen covering the joint digital organ venture goes into some detail as to the rights of the two parties regarding the patents resulting from the development effort. As stated in the contracts,

> NR, insofar as it has a right to do so, during the life of any patent which may issue on said Patent Application Serial No. 660,997 or of none issues, for a period of ten (10) years from the effective date hereof, hereby grants to Allen...a right of first refusal at a price and on terms and conditions to be agreed upon for an exclusive license, with the right to sublicense, within the Field in any patent or patent application filed by NR subsequent to the date of this agreement, in the United States, United Kingdom, Federal Republic of Germany, France, Italy, the Netherlands, Japan, Switzerland and Belgium, to make, use and sell Items incorporating any of the following made by Autonetics personnel working in the Field:
>
> (1) Any new electronic musical instrument system in which tones are manually selected;
>
> (2) Any invention which is primarily useful in the generation of music by means of an electronic musical instrument in which tones are manually selected; and

(3) Any invention the use of which necessarily infringes one or more claims as contained in Patent Application No. 660,997 as of April 2, 1969.

Cutting through the legalese of the contract language, the essence of the above agreement between Rockwell (NR) and Allen was that Allen, who was paying for the development, had a "right of first refusal" to any technology developed by Rockwell (Autonetics) relating to the joint venture. The agreement, as stated, covered a very long period of time (at least ten years). Clearly, we expected the relationship between the two companies to go on for a long time. Rockwell would have developed the basic technology; Allen would convert the technology into viable musical products and market the products based on that technology.

The patent application No. 660,997 eventually resulted in a patent. In addition, several other key patents also eventually resulted from the development effort. All of these are the basic patents in the digital musical instrument field. These instruments could not be designed without infringing on some aspect covered by these basic patents. The good part about this situation for Allen was the fact that Allen "controlled" the digital musical instrument field by virtue of its "right of first refusal" as stipulated in the original contracts as described above. The bad part, in a sense, is that the dramatic success of the digital organ technology put Allen in the position of being a roadblock to Ralph

Deutsch. Unwittingly, Allen was (and perhaps still is) the target of Deutsch's manifold meddling. The main consequences of this meddling to Allen has, so far, been lost revenue because of legal expenses, and possibly some lost sales. To a degree, his actions also gave the Japanese a head start in the digital musical instrument field. Let me elaborate on the Japanese connection.

The computer organ was shown at the National Association of Music Merchants (NAMM) Show in June of 1971, causing quite a stir. Early on in the show, Deutsch asked me whether I'd mind giving a private demonstration of the organ to the president of Yamaha. Since we had an open-door policy to any and all visitors to our showroom who wanted a demonstration, I agreed to Deutsch's request with some uneasiness. At the appointed time, after regular show hours, we were indeed visited not only by Deutsch and Genichi Kawakami, president of Yamaha, but also by Kawakami's overwhelming entourage of twenty-five-or-so Japanese associates. After observing what they could about the computer organ, the Japanese group had quite a spirited conversation in Japanese. As I recall it, Jim Kagawa, a Rockwell employee acting as interpreter, reported to us that Kawakami had berated his people for not coming up with something like the digital organ, saying something equivalent to, "If you guys can't give us what we want, we'll get the technology from someone else."

I didn't find out until several years later that shortly after the NAMM Show Deutsch disclosed the detailed workings of the computer organ to Yamaha's engineering management without Allen's knowledge and certainly without Allen's approval. Also, I must note that there is a vital difference between demonstrating the "operation" of one's product to the public and disclosing, in great detail, "how to build" the product. And I'm talking about a very complex, revolutionary new technology. Obviously, telling a competitor how to build such a product would be considered unthinkable. I must be clear about another thing. I bear no animosity towards Yamaha for taking something that was handed to them on a platter.

Going back to '71, right after the NAMM Show, I got a call from Deutsch indicating that Yamaha was interested in applying the new technology to a small organ. He requested that I have a conference with some Yamaha people whom he would accompany to our plant in Macungie. I hesitatingly agreed to hear what they had to say. On July 19, 1971, Deutsch along with a Rockwell vice president and the Japanese representatives arrived for the meeting. We discussed the subject as planned but were unable to come to terms. After the meeting, we heard no more from Deutsch or Yamaha aside from a follow-up letter from Genichi Kawakami.

Again, much later, I found out that following the July 19 meeting, Deutsch continued to court the Japanese and eventually engaged in secret negotiations with Yamaha about shifting his allegiance and talents to Japan. This took place while he was still on the Rockwell payroll. Of course, Allen knew nothing about Deutsch's maneuvering at the time; perhaps Rockwell didn't either. As is now well known, in the early 1970s, Japan was heavily engaged in the importation of high technology into their country with an eye towards the eventual exportation of products based on that technology. In the musical instrument field, Deutsch was a willing collaborator in this plan. For Yamaha, today the world's largest manufacturer of musical instruments, Deutsch provided the "fast track" route for getting into the new digital technology. Indeed, Deutsch visited Japan and Yamaha three or four times in the latter part of 1971.

Although the details are somewhat shrouded in mystery, Deutsch left Rockwell in early January, 1972, and entered into a three-year agreement with Yamaha on April 30, 1972, to be a digital musical instrument consultant. To top it off, he applied for a new digital organ patent on February 14, 1972, less than six weeks after leaving Rockwell; yet, he swore under oath that the new invention had no connection at all to his working for Rockwell (and Allen) just six weeks before applying for the patent. Anyone familiar with high-tech patents would doubt Deutsch's explanation. The final patent ran over fifteen pages of fine print including the required and detailed explanation of the system and how it works along with diagrams, lists of parts used in construction, precisely defined legal claims, etc. The carefully-worded pronouncements quoted previously from the original Allen-Rockwell contracts concerning a minimum ten-year commitment to Allen's rights to the new technology had apparently meant nothing to Deutsch either legally or morally. Capitalizing on his privileged position, he took payments from Yamaha for three years in return for his specialized knowledge. After the three-year contract expired, Deutsch tried to renew it, but Yamaha had learned enough to carry on with the new technology by themselves and bid Deutsch farewell. Since then Yamaha has applied for more United States' patents than any other company in the musical instrument field.

Litigations

In the chapter entitled, "Patents and Intellectual Property," I briefly discussed the concept of intellectual property and the need for laws to protect both inventors and society with regard to the exploitation of new technology. I then talked about patents and the patent laws as the specific means by which we can deal with these issues.

Patents and patent laws vary somewhat from country to country. How the citizens of a society behave with regard to patents and the patent laws also varies from country to country. I've read, for example, that the United States has many more attorneys per capita than Japan. This would suggest that in our society disputes end up in court more frequently than they do in Japan. I wonder, along with many others, why this is so.

Are Americans more aggressive than Japanese? Do Americans view the law as something to "beat" rather than uphold? Do the Japanese place more value on maintaining good, personal relationships through voluntary cooperation than do the Americans? We could go on and ask more questions, but my interest in raising these few is not so much aimed at the larger sociological view as it is toward my own experience with litigations over the years.

In contemplating the history of Allen Organ Company, I have to address the fact that Allen has been involved in more than a dozen litigations. In my view as a businessman, even one litigation is too many. Resources are diverted away from projects aimed at improving productivity and end up in the hands of lawyers. For this reason, litigation is, in my opinion, counterproductive to our national interests. How on earth, then, did Allen Organ become involved in so many lawsuits?

In addressing the above question I will present my recollections of some of these cases and offer some commentary. In the final analysis, you will, I'm sure, draw your own conclusions about these very complex issues.

As I went back in time mentally "reliving" each case, I realized how much emotion and drama surrounded each one. Believe me, being grilled under oath is a good test of one's mettle. Rerunning these scenarios in my mind is a little like reading Shakespeare's plays. The scenes are set up. The characters are introduced—villains, heroes, innocent

victims, troublemakers, etc. The stories unfold
sometimes tragically, sometimes humorously, but always
"interestingly."

HAYGREN ORGAN COMPANY

In the summer of 1948, Allen Organ Company first
exhibited at a National Association of Music
Manufacturers convention in Chicago. The product
shown was one of our 1948 tube organs which included
a special rack construction which was granted U.S.
Patent 2,495,339 on January 24, 1950. The patented
aspects of the rack construction dealt mainly with
conveniences to the service technician.

During this showing, we met many interested parties
including two bright young chaps from the Chicago
area named Richard Peterson and Soloman Heytow.
They indicated an interest in servicing our products,
which were then being sold in the Chicago area through
a dealer in Fort Wayne, Indiana. According to my best
recollection, they indeed did some repairs of our
products through contacts with the Fort Wayne dealer.

By around 1950, they were operating their own
company, Haygren Organ Company, and proceeded to
manufacture organs using technology similar to ours.
Upon examination, the structure of their tone generator
racks strongly resembled that of ours. After discussing
this with an attorney, we were advised that Haygren
was infringing on our U.S. Patent 2,495,339. "Notice"
letters, which are usual in such situations, were ignored;

therefore, in February, 1952, we instituted a Complaint charging patent infringement.

For those unfamiliar with the term "discovery," it is the procedure of gathering information and of taking sworn testimony (depositions) prior to a trial. In the Haygren case, discovery was ongoing through approximately August, 1953, at which time Haygren agreed to cease the practice in question. We sought no damages and were satisfied that the situation was resolved.

Subsequently, Richard Peterson approached me for a private meeting; in a hotel room in Chicago, he castigated me for filing the lawsuit against Haygren. I tried to explain my perception of what a patent was all about, but I'm not sure that I got through. The thing that always troubled me was that the infringing part of their apparatus was not really basic to the sales features of their organs. They could have easily circumvented infringement concerns in various ways only affecting convenience to the service technician.

CHORAL AND ORGAN GUIDE MAGAZINE
(Roy Anderson)

During the late 1950s, Roy Anderson published and edited a small-size, periodically-issued magazine covering items of interest to organists and those involved in choral work. In one issue of the magazine, a complimentary article about Allen Organ Company and its products appeared. This article was in no way solicited by either me or any of my associates but was rather initiated by Mr. Anderson.

Subsequently, we were solicited for advertising by Mr. Anderson. I then began to pay more attention to this publication and noted with interest that it had begun to attack the Hammond Organ Company and its product. My initial reaction was that Anderson had selected our product for its superior qualities as a focus for complimentary editorial content. But this was not a valid conclusion.

Shortly thereafter he attacked Moller, a prominent pipe organ manufacturer. Around the same time his "pressure" for advertising from our Company increased. It was then that I learned about publications which employ carrot and stick routines with potential advertisers. Give them some favorable commentary or publicity, pressure them for advertising, and "sock it to them" if the companies do not respond.

Well, this indeed occurred. In the February, 1960, issue of *Choral and Organ Guide*, Anderson struck at Allen Organ Company with a grossly inaccurate description of certain events which were alleged to have occurred in the relationship between Allen Organ Company and one of its dealers in Illinois.

We instructed our attorney to warn him to cease these activities. His arrogant response was the printing of the letter from our attorney in the magazine. It seemed like he was out to intimidate the entire industry.

At this point, some inner sense of indignation then impelled us to file a lawsuit charging libel in early 1960.

Discovery promptly followed and consisted of two depositions in which Mr. Anderson was interrogated under oath. It turned out that many of his representations would, almost surely, be a serious problem for him in a court of law. I suspect that his attorney advised him to settle. Consequently, in the January, 1961, issue of his magazine, he essentially retracted the statements and admitted error. These actions put the matter to rest; we heard no more from Mr. Anderson. However, I am not sure why we never received a word of thanks from either of the two companies that he had previously attacked.

RODGERS ORGAN COMPANY

During my study of pipe organs in the late 1950s, I discovered that many organ pipes were characterized by a sort of accent at the beginning of the speech of the pipe, sometimes called chiff. Subsequently, I received some U. S. Patents in the early 1960s including No. 3,037,413 describing a type of circuitry for implementing chiff in an electronic organ.

Prior to this, somewhere in 1956 or 1957, we were visited at our factory by Rodgers Jenkins. He seemed to be a technically precocious young man and indicated an interest in servicing our instruments in the Portland, Oregon, area. Later, he established some relationship with our Portland dealer, and I believe that we provided him with various servicing information.

Around 1958, Rodgers Organ Company was formed and began manufacturing organs in the Portland area, producing instruments basically similar to ours. By about 1963, they incorporated a chiff feature in their products. After investigation, we were convinced, along with our attorneys, that there indeed was an infringement. After some warning letters which were ignored, we instituted suit for patent infringement in June of 1964.

The first focus of their discovery was the taking of my deposition on September 29, 1964. At the end of the testimony, their attorney indicated a willingness to settle the case. This occurred with Rodgers providing us with a relatively small but meaningful royalty payment each year for the life of the patent, which expired in 1979.

ROCKWELL INTERNATIONAL

In 1972, there was a build-up of differences between Allen and Rockwell relating to certain aspects of the ongoing, joint venture. Unable to resolve these differences, Allen sued Rockwell in August, 1972. The case came to trial in 1976, and during trial it was settled. The settlement agreement between the parties, among other things, indicated that Allen would not exploit the matter in any manner that would be detrimental to Rockwell. With this in mind, my only comment is that various newspapers articles appeared at the time reflecting what, in the opinion of my associates and me, was a favorable resolution for Allen.

Moreover, as far as Allen is concerned, the matter was settled and is over and done with, and the details of the matter need not be further discussed.

However, an important point to note is that included in the agreement was the transmission of the ownership of certain patents from Rockwell to Allen which later turned out to be a mixed blessing, although mainly positive.

YAMAHA (NIPPON-GAKKI)

As early as 1974, we discussed with Yamaha possible conflict between one or more of the "Rockwell" patents and Yamaha's plans for the development of products for the electronic music field. Eventually, these communications included meetings at Allen's factory in Macungie, Pennsylvania, and culminated in a virtual licensing agreement by April, 1977. However, I was convinced that as a matter of "honor" or respect I should travel to Japan to meet with Yamaha's highest officials so that the contract could be properly finalized and "inked." Therefore, on May 21, 1977, I flew to Japan along with Anthony Volpe, an attorney whom we had employed. We were met at the airport by Mr. Yasunori Mochida, a director and high official of Yamaha whom we had met on previous occasions. He escorted us via bullet train to Hamamatsu, a city situated between Tokyo and Osaka.

Since our arrival was on a Sunday, we were told that we would meet on Monday morning for the purpose of viewing Yamaha's facilities. In addition, we were told to take it easy for the remaining portion of Monday because Mochida specifically suggested that he wanted us to have an opportunity to get rid of jet lag before being involved in the contract matters.

Early Monday morning we were picked up by Mr. Mochida and taken to Yamaha's formidable manufacturing plant on the outskirts of Hamamatsu. During the next few hours we were duly impressed by their capabilities. At approximately 11:00 A.M., we were invited into one of the conference rooms. After some tea and cookies, as I recall, we received our first surprise. We were joined by additional Yamaha personnel. I am not sure just which of them said essentially, "Let's start talking." This gave us a bit of discomfort because it was still only Monday, and we expected only to be resting on Monday following the long flight from the United States. Under the circumstances, we had no choice but to either protest or "start talking." I thought the discussions would be merely pro forma. Therefore, I decided that we would go along with the Japanese and wrap up the discussions without further delay.

The Yamaha people then began haggling over various minor details that were to be worked into the agreement. This surprised us because we thought these matters had been settled before we left the United

States. Further, as stated previously, our only purpose in going to Japan was for the diplomatic aspects involved; if the Japanese had spent substantial time and money in coming to the United States for discussions with us, we should reciprocate with at least one trip to Japan.

Later we had some lunch, and the haggling continued. Then, at approximately 3:00 P.M. a bombshell hit! We were told that a courier had just arrived from the United States with documents which would show that at least one patent was invalid. By this time both Volpe and I, getting more uncomfortable by the minute and not fully recovered from the jet lag, began showing the effects of the strain. Volpe blew up and began berating the Japanese for pulling what appeared to be a cheap trick. Subsequently, we regained our composures and, by about an hour later, had prepared a rough document covering a license agreement.

Just about this time, Hiroshi Kawakami, the son of President Genichi Kawakami, entered the conference room and began looking over the documents. He seemed angry; with a dramatic flourish, he took his pen and made a big "X" across the document thus indicating his extreme disapproval. At this point, the meeting was approaching chaos; but, again, things quieted down. After approximately an hour or so, we indeed had a rough document which was agreed to by the parties. The document was reflective of what was later to be converted into a formal document by the joint agreement of Allen and Yamaha attorneys. Things were now on an even keel and we were treated to a fine dinner prior to retiring for the evening.

Our patent business was now concluded. Therefore, I decided that I would take advantage of the fact that, in order to go back to the United States, a return to Tokyo was necessary. Realizing there were several hours of waiting involved, I decided that I would go to the U. S. Yokota Air Base near Tokyo where an Allen Organ had been installed in the main military chapel. The Yamaha people kindly provided me with one of their engineers who acted as a guide back to Tokyo and then to the Air Base where we had a very pleasant visit.

I believe that it was on Thursday morning, May 26, that I returned to my office to resume the various routine business matters at hand. My associates and I were certainly not ready for the bombshell being sent our way.

On June 2, 1977, by registered mail, we were served with a Complaint, Yamaha vs. Allen, in the form of a Motion for Declaratory Judgment asserting invalidity of at least one of the patents. The Complaint was approximately eighteen pages long; I was surprised that this formidable document had arrived so promptly after my return from Japan.

A "Declaratory Judgment" action, for those who are not familiar with the term, is a lawsuit initiated by someone who allegedly is threatened by a potential plaintiff. The purpose is to seize the initiative before the plaintiff acts. Of course, in this situation, we had no intention of filing a lawsuit since we thought that we had already settled the matter.

Consternation followed. However, we reacted quickly. Within the next few days we filed a countersuit charging Yamaha, among other things, with patent infringement and violation of antitrust laws.

As the summer of 1977 moved on, it became apparent that Yamaha really was not too anxious to pursue the litigation. Settlement discussions occurred after Yamaha switched lawyers, the case being taken over by a Japanese-American lawyer named Jun Mori. After this change, dealings became much more pleasant. By October, a settlement was reached with the situation being reported in the *Wall Street Journal* on November 3, 1977.

The settlement included a payment by Yamaha to Allen of a minimum of $1 million and a maximum of $2,250,000 over a five-year period in return for settlement of the litigation and a license to continue manufacturing electronic musical instruments using the patents.

The settlement was actually more favorable than that which we had agreed upon in Japan. I can only speculate that some U.S. lawyers had convinced Yamaha that they could break the patent or patents, and Yamaha later had second thoughts. In any case, subsequently Yamaha fulfilled all of their obligations in a timely manner. Other than the frenetic events which occurred early on, I can't say that I maintain any malice toward them.

KLANN ORGAN COMPANY

Let us return to the Allen vs. Rockwell litigation which, as previously indicated, covered the period of 1972 through 1976. On May 10, 1974, to the great surprise of both Allen and Rockwell, both parties were served with a patent infringement complaint by Klann Organ Company, a relatively small producer of organ supplies in Virginia. Strangely enough, this suit was initiated in the Central District of California, Los Angeles. "Discovery" proceedings followed.

Sometimes during discovery either or both sides obtain a better picture of their position—whether stronger or weaker— than they originally perceived. This often leads to a settlement prior to trial. A most unusual aspect of this case, brought to light through the deposition of Paul Klann, president of Klann Organ Company, was the identity of the lawyer in California who represented him and the circumstances surrounding how it came to pass that Klann selected an attorney so remote from Klann's business establishment.

What was "discovered" was that during a trip to the West Coast, Paul Klann had, among other things, met with none other than Ralph Deutsch. While not directly admitted, it seemed to me that Deutsch germinated this litigation by saying whatever it took to incite Klann to file the suit. To make the matter even simpler for Klann, Deutsch accompanied him to another office in the same building to obtain the services of Attorney Howard Silber.

Interestingly, attorney Silber was the very same attorney who was previously employed by Rockwell in the 1967-68 time frame as an in-house patent attorney working on the original digital organ patents. In view of this, Rockwell immediately took legal steps to have Klann's attorney, Howard Silber, disqualified on the basis of conflict of interest due to his previous employment at Rockwell. This procedure was successful; in September, Silber was indeed disqualified and the case was dismissed. This means that the issues of the Complaint were never tried by the court. In the years following, Klann chose not to exercise his option to revive the litigation with another attorney. Shakespeare might have called this case "much ado about nothing."

OTHER JAPANESE COMPANIES

During 1981, we became aware of another Japanese company which we believed was infringing on certain of our patents. Again, a series of notice letters was forwarded; since these did not produce any results, we felt compelled to institute a patent-infringement lawsuit shortly thereafter.

This lawsuit went through the initial stages of discovery; then, it became apparent that the company involved would be willing to settle. The settlement

included an up-front payment to Allen. My reason for
not identifying this particular company is that, as
reflected in the settlement agreement, confidentiality
was required at the insistence of the licensee. I never
fully understood the rationale for secrecy since,
ultimately, the terms had to be disclosed in our financial
statements. In any case, I have no desire to breach the
agreement.

In the period following this settlement, additional
license agreements were negotiated with other Japanese
companies including Roland, Akai, Matsushita, Seiko,
and Korg. These license agreements were negotiated on
a "business basis" without any litigation. I believe that
the terms of the agreements reflected our appreciation
for the avoidance of litigation.

Losing
a Patent

In a recent article, *Electronic Business* magazine wrote about the necessity for companies in the electronics industry to take action to protect their intellectual property. The article states:

> Losses from intellectual property theft have been staggering. According to an International Trade Commission study, in which 31 computer and software makers participated, $4.1 billion was lost in the computer and software industries in 1986 due to intellectual property infringement. About $271 million was spent on enforcement of intellectual property rights by the 199 companies, from all industries, that answered the ITC survey.[1]

---

[1]Reprinted with permission from ELECTRONIC BUSINESS, September 15, 1988 ©1988 by Cahners Publishing Company

Clearly, Allen Organ is not alone in having to protect itself from problems with its intellectual property.

In reviewing our track record in protecting our intellectual property rights, I conclude that we've been generally successful. In almost all of the disputes in which we've been involved over the years—not only those concerning intellectual property rights but those involving other matters as well—we have been able to attain what I feel is a fair resolution. However, one glaring exception, where we failed in our effort to protect our intellectual property, does exist. This is a case mainly involving the Watson U. S. Patent 3,610,799. I believe it would be useful to focus a little more attention on this case to find out how we lost this "property."

After the Allen vs. Rockwell case was settled in 1976, Allen obtained ownership of various Rockwell patents relating to the digital organ project, including U. S. Patent 3,610,799. This is one of the landmark patents in the history of electronic musical instrument design. It is so basic that I could hardly conceive of any musical instrument with a digital keyboard that would not infringe this patent in some way. Because many companies would be following our lead into the "digital keyboard" revolution, it was important for us to protect ourselves against the theft of this valuable property.

No doubt existed that theft could take place. All we had to do was look around. By the 1980s, digital keyboard instruments were turning up all over the place. However, in 1976, I felt completely confident that we were protected by the law of the land, i.e. the patent laws.

The Allen-Rockwell joint venture had resulted in the invention of the new digital technology for building keyboard instruments. This technology was patented; after 1976, Allen owned the patents. In theory, while a patent means that others could be prevented from using it, we chose to notify alleged infringers and then negotiate reasonable license agreements with them. Our objective was to "sell" the right to use our technology, via fair licensing, to as many companies as would want to use it. We had hoped the many license fees coming in would add up to a respectable return on all the investments we, ourselves, had made in the new technology over the years.

To the best of my knowledge, most if not all of the companies we dealt with had lawyers scrutinize the validity of our rights after we notified them about potential infringement. Apparently based on the strength of our position, some of these companies expeditiously decided to go along with our economical licensing plan and get on with their business without further infringement concerns. With the collapse of the home organ market, beginning in 1979, a few other companies succumbed before inking a licensing agreement with us. In addition, a few companies tested our resolve—we had to engage in some litigation before they decided that licensing the technology made the most business sense. However, one company, Kimball International, a large Indiana manufacturer of pianos, organs, and furniture, chose a different course.

In early 1977, we opened communications with Kimball to address the likely possibility that there was infringement of the Watson patent. Based on the ensuing discussions, the only real issue appeared to be the magnitude of the licensing fee. However, various other events and proposals complicated what first seemed to be an otherwise straightforward business deal. In fact, we found ourselves still "discussing" the matter with Kimball more than a year later.

Then, on May 23, 1978, without a hint of warning, we were served with legal papers. They represented a Motion for Declaratory Judgment filed by Kimball and asserted that the patent was invalid for so many alleged reasons that the whole tactic seemed to be simply ludicrous. In plain English, Kimball had sued us. We, of course, had to immediately countersue them for patent infringement—the best way, we thought, to protect ourselves in court. The whole thing didn't make much sense to us. The patent had already been exposed to much scrutiny by that time; I thought that Kimball's chances of breaking such a solid patent were slim or nonexistent.

There's another point I'd like to make about Kimball's tactic. Patent litigation is enormously expensive. I knew that under such circumstances

Kimball's legal fees would quickly exceed what we were asking for a license, even if they didn't bother to negotiate the price downward. The suit seemed to me to be a nonsensical waste of money. I still cannot figure out any reason for Kimball's aggressive litigation tactic other than to simply "punish" Allen. Their action did exact a toll on us; our resources were diverted from productive activities to legal-defense activities. The litigation dragged on for years; however, the biggest blow came at the end—we lost.

As an aside, it is instructive to compare what I viewed as Kimball's aggressive litigation tactic with the approach taken by the Japanese companies. All of the Japanese companies we approached about licensing chose to limit the money they spent on arguing or litigating. Instead, they obtained licenses and concentrated their time and energy on product development. I believe this is one main reason why the Japanese presently dominate most of the musical instrument industry while most of the older American companies either have gone out of business, have been "restructured," or have been purchased by foreign companies.

In retrospect, how did Kimball "beat" what I thought was a seemingly air-tight patent? To answer this question, let's take time to go over some important rules associated with our patent system before I recount the story in greater detail.

In the United States, a patent is a legal monopoly granted by the government for a period of seventeen years. During this period, the patent owner may either retain exclusive rights to the use of the invention, or license others to use the invention on terms of his choosing.

Many have the misconception that a patent automatically prevents others from manufacturing a product covered by the patent. In actuality, the grant of a patent merely is a license to sue infringers. Moreover, a patent can be taken away, i.e., invalidated, even after it is granted by the Patent Office. In fact, many opportunities exist in our legal system to defeat a patent through invalidation. First, a patent can be invalidated if it is determined that the inventor withheld information from the Patent Office when the patent application was filed. Second, a patent can be invalidated if the invention described in the patent is put on sale prior to twelve months before the date of the application. Third, invalidation can occur if the patented idea would have been obvious to anyone skilled in the art when the idea was conceived. Fourth, a patent is invalid if the invention is publicly disclosed prior to twelve months before the date of the application.

With this general background established, I can now go into a little more detail as to what took place in our dealings with Kimball, as I recall it.

At the end of 1976, we approached Kimball about the possibility of their infringing one or more of the digital organ patents.

We also expressed our desire to license the new technology. Immediately we were contacted by their attorney, Albert Jeffers, who suggested that he would like to visit with us to discuss the matter.

On February 16, 1977, a pleasant meeting occurred. The meeting was attended by our attorney, Anthony Volpe, Attorney Jeffers and his associate patent agent, and me. Jeffers explained that Kimball was adverse to paying royalties but they might consider a "paid-up" license. This type of arrangement can simply be described as a single, one-time payment for the right to use a patent or patents. No necessity exists for reporting the number of units sold, etc., as is required in the case of a royalty arrangement. The paid-up license arrangement did not seem unreasonable to me.

Keeping in mind our policy of offering reasonable terms so as to discourage litigation, I suggested a flat payment of $400,000. Based upon our impression of Kimball's production and anticipated production, this would have only amounted to perhaps one dollar per organ; retail prices of such organs ranged from approximately $500 to $5,000. The figure quoted was an "asking" amount; as this was to be our "first" license agreement of the digital organ technology, I was ready to negotiate. Jeffers stated that he would take the proposition back to Kimball management and that he would be in further contact with us.

In the meantime, Yamaha filed their Declaratory Judgment against us on June 2, 1977. Our attorney wrote to Kimball notifying them about the Yamaha vs. Allen litigation, suggesting that we cease negotiations until the Yamaha case was resolved. We stated that we believed that our case was very strong and we still intended to maintain all rights to the technology— pending the outcome of the litigation with Yamaha.

In spite of our backing off from the negotiations, Attorney Jeffers requested a meeting at his offices in Fort Wayne, Indiana. The meeting occurred on June 24, 1977, attended by Attorney Volpe and my son, Steven Markowitz. Steven had recently graduated from Penn State University, joined the company, and was taking on some important missions—primarily the spearheading of our major thrust into the international marketplace.

Upon their return, Attorney Volpe and Steven reported that Jeffers was very cordial and friendly and even assured them that Kimball would never do what Yamaha did—force us into court without warning via a Declaratory Judgment Motion. Our licensing proposal was, supposedly, still being taken under advisement by Kimball.

In the fall of 1977, I received a communication from an investment banker, Joseph Ponce, with whom I was acquainted, indicating that Kimball was interested in discussing a merger with Allen Organ Company. I was not too thrilled with this prospect and did not respond enthusiastically. However, subsequent communications from Mr. Ponce followed. He indicated that Kimball was very serious about this idea. As he laid out the benefits of such a merger, my associates and I did not feel that their proposal could be ignored. On January 19, 1978, we were visited by Arnold Habig, chairman of Kimball, and Mr. Ponce; a snow storm prevented certain other representatives of Kimball from attending. At the end of the visit, Mr. Habig appeared quite impressed with our operation.

Kimball's courting efforts continued, in early 1978, far away from our plant in Macungie. My son, Steven, had organized an Allen exhibit at the Frankfurt Music Fair, Europe's biggest gathering place for the showing of products by manufacturers of music-related equipment. While at the Fair, Steven was approached by Kimball. Mr. Habig wanted to talk and invited Steven to dinner. Steven agreed and later met Mr. Habig at Habig's headquarters in Frankfurt. As Steven later described the incident to me, Habig's accommodations were opulent compared to what Steven was used to. Steven had the impression that he was in the presence of someone who was intimately familiar with corporate power. As the amenities faded into the nitty-gritty, Mr. Habig suggested to Steven that a merger between Kimball and Allen would be good for Steven's career.

Habig went on to imply that Steven could receive a position of "power" within the combined enterprise.

I suppose Habig had hoped that Steven, young and ambitious, just might jump at such an alluring prospect and use his influence with me to help bring about the merger of the two companies—thus getting himself on an easy fast-track to fame and fortune. Of course, Steven did not respond to this approach but rather promptly reported the incident to us.

A second meeting was held at our plant on April 12, 1978. This meeting was again attended by Kimball chairman, Arnold Habig, along with Joseph Ponce and other Kimball executives. As the discussion progressed into the evening hours, it seemed that there were differences between us. The Kimball people left with Mr. Habig urging that we consider visiting their establishment in southern Indiana where he felt that we could be impressed enough to give more serious consideration to their proposals.

Interestingly, we had settled the patent litigation with Yamaha by this time and could have reopened the patent negotiations with Kimball. However, I chose to allow the patent negotiations with Kimball to remain in suspension. I felt it would be improper to pressure Kimball about patent infringement matters when they wanted to talk about the broader merger issue.

In the days following, I attempted to phone Mr. Habig to set a date for our visit to their facility, but I had difficulty getting through to him. After several days

I finally did reach him. From excuses he offered regarding unavailability of personnel, etc., I sensed something had changed in Habig's attitude; so, I decided that it would be well to let the matter drop. This all was occurring in April; therefore, my associates and I were hardly prepared for what happened in May!

On May 23, 1978, we were served with Kimball's Motion for Declaratory Judgment in which Kimball put forth each and every possible attack on the patent. They alleged the patent was obtained by fraud since Rockwell had allegedly withheld information from the Patent Office. Further, they alleged that the invention would have been obvious to anybody skilled in the art. In addition, they alleged that it was on sale more than twelve months prior to the filing of the application. In other words, they put forth a total package of allegations any single one of which would, if true, be a cause for invalidation of the patent. The barrage of allegations came as quite a shock because we had just recently met with the Kimball people—in meetings which they had initiated in connection with the proposed merger.

As previously stated, patent litigation is an expensive procedure; therefore, it seemed difficult to believe that Kimball would rather pay more to litigate than simply obtain a license without the bother of lawsuit. I kept mulling it over in my mind, searching for some rationale. Did they have some "ace-in-the-hole" evidence of which we weren't aware? Did they have some special strategy which we were not able to perceive?

Moving back for the moment to early 1978, we also attempted to enforce the George Watson U. S. Patent 3,610,799 against Conn Organ Company. A substantial interchange of correspondence first occurred with no productive results. Consequently, on February 14, 1978, we filed suit against Conn Organ Company in which we cited patent infringement.

The Conn case began moving along slowly until 1981, at which time Kimball arrived at an agreement with Conn Organ Company's parent company, Macmillan, the publisher, to acquire Conn, thus merging the two companies. After that, Kimball and its attorneys took over the Allen vs. Conn case from Macmillan. Discovery plodded along in this combined Allen/Kimball/Conn imbroglio. For almost seven years, paper work piled up from correspondence, from depositions, and from other evidence produced by discovery. All told, we are talking about thousands of pages of material.

In my opinion, some lawyers have a way of turning a relatively straightforward issue into a morass of obfuscation. I'm still troubled when I look back at the huge pile of material generated as a result of this case.

To continue about the actual Kimball vs. Allen litigation, the trial itself began on October 7, 1985. In the end the jury decided against Allen. The case then went to the Appeals Court, which rendered a final decision also against Allen. The case began in 1978, and the final Appeals Court decision was rendered in 1988. Incredibly, it took almost ten years to crawl through this legal quagmire.

The sad thing is that the patent had passed the "real" tests of merit—other than two of the thirty-six patent claims, the jury found it to be a truly inventive idea. Moreover, they found it to be a non-obvious idea at the time it was conceived. What was actually used to invalidate the patent was an alleged breaking of a rule having to do with how the patent application was filed. As Kimball was trying to establish this part of their case before the jury, I found it to be so implausible that I took for granted that the jury would also find it to be so. This was a gross mistake on my part.

Once again, Ralph Deutsch had resurfaced—this time in the Kimball case. During the trial he testified as Kimball's witness and admitted that his fee was $1,000 per day. Deutsch, under oath, testified that all of the elements of Watson's invention were present in the "demonstrator," the special apparatus which Rockwell assembled to demonstrate the sound of the proposed digital organ. Deutsch, the digital organ program manager, had shown the "demonstrator" to people at various organ companies in his quest to find a company willing to fund the program—he was seeking an arrangement which would ultimately lead to the development of the actual digital organ. This is the apparatus which I went to see in California in 1968.

Patent law states that one can't get a patent on an invention if it is put on sale or in public use more than one year before filing the patent application. In fact, the inventor must swear under oath that the invention was not in public use or "on sale" more than one year before filing. As part of Kimball's broad-brush attack of the patent, they alleged that the invention covered by the patent was "on sale" and in public use in the form of the "demonstrator" more than one year before the patent application was filed. If one were to read the section of the trial transcript dealing with this allegation, I believe it would be agreed that Kimball and its witnesses made every effort to give the impression that the "invention" was in public use and "on sale" when Deutsch went around to the organ companies to solicit development money. I believe that there was a great deal of confusion and uncertainty about what the witnesses were really saying. However, given the confusing testimony and the complexity of the issue, the jury ended up agreeing with Kimball's allegation much to my shocked dismay. Thus, the trial ended on November 6, 1985. Aside from appealing, the patent was lost. This was a bitter pill to swallow even though the patent's seventeen-year life was due to expire anyway on October 5, 1988.

After the initial shock of the verdict wore off, I realized that the trial had turned into a fiasco. However, I still had every confidence that it would all be straightened out by the Appeals Court. I was told that the Appeals Court consisted of judges who not only knew the law but also were trained to understand the complex technical issues often encountered in patent cases. So, off to the Appeals Court in Washington, D.C., we went. After more than two years of anticipating a ruling in our favor, the Appeals Court finally delivered their judgment on February 12, 1988. I was horrified! These sages of justice simply rubber-stamped the jury's confused findings. Now it was final. We had lost the patent.

There's no space here to go into much detail about why I feel so frustrated about the results of this case. But permit me to present a few facts so you can judge for yourself.

Here is a direct quote from Deutsch taken under oath at a deposition on October 29, 1979:

> "Claim 22 which refers back to Claim 19 talks about, 'a need of producing transient percussion control signal.' It also talks about a percussion means responsive to that signal. That was not on the demonstrator. In fact, was done on the engineering model. And there are a couple of other claims, I think 23 — any claim that refers to this — I believe it refers to the percussion control signal in Claim 23 was not in the demonstrator."

This is a plain statement saying that the allegedly on-sale "demonstrator" did <u>not</u> contain the aspects of the invention which dealt with the keying of "percussive" instruments—specifically claims number 4, 22, 23, 32, and 33.

Now, below is quoted a portion of the Appeals Court judgment:

> "Careful review of the record, necessitated by the parties' combined challenge to the entire trial process, shows substantial evidence in support of the jury's presumed finding that the demonstrator embodied all the '799 patent claims including the percussive claims. For example, Deutsch, inventor of the '806 patent and an employee at Rockwell, testified 'all these claims [percussive claims 4, 22, 23, 32 and 33] read on the demonstrator.' "

Here are other direct quotes from Deutsch taken under oath at the trial:

> "the demonstrator was never on sale itself." (Trial transcript, page 1277, line 19)

> "I have never testified we were selling the demonstrator." (Trial transcript, page 1278, lines 18 and 19)

Astonishingly, the Appeals Court further stated in their judgment:

> "The record also shows substantial evidence on which a reasonable jury could have found the demonstrator to have been in public use and on sale, and that the use was not primarily experimental."

Forces Influencing the Organ's Destiny

Pipe organs have been evolving over the last three thousand years. With this rich heritage, they have retained a position among the traditional keyboard instruments. However, a dispassionate eye would have to see that the role of the pipe organ, within the larger cultural framework, has subtly changed over the years.

By the Baroque period, the pipe organ had earned the title, "King of Instruments." One can imagine the emotional impact on the listeners of that time as they sat in the splendor of Baroque churches and cathedrals in various parts of Europe. However, by the 1800s, challengers to the mighty pipe organ appeared on the scene, including the symphony orchestra and the piano. As the nineteenth century unfolded, the formerly predominant position of the pipe organ as a musical instrument had to be reactive to the onslaught of the newcomers. In a sense, organists and organ aficionados were forced to become a breed apart from the mainstream of the musical world, which included the piano and violin as primary solo instruments and the symphony orchestra as the preferred unit for recreating the works of the masters. The fact that the pipe organ still plays a role in today's musical world is a tribute to the tenacity of the organ enthusiasts of the last century.

Today, pressures on the pipe organ as a viable instrument have intensified. For example, there is simple economic pressure. The cost to construct and maintain a pipe organ has skyrocketed. A potentially good pipe organ can cost over one million dollars. I say "potentially good" because there is certainly no guarantee that a newly built pipe organ will perform up to expectations. Moreover, customers footing the bill for these expensive "shots-in-the-dark" are rebelling.

Another economic reality is felt by organists directly. Today, a concert pianist of recognized stature can command a fee many times greater than that of an organist of comparable musical stature. This economic discrimination has only increased the isolation of organists from the mainstream.

Other factors have dampened the pipe organ's effectiveness as a musical instrument. We don't build as many mammoth cathedrals of stone as we did formerly. Instead, we build churches, auditoriums, concert halls, etc., using modern materials such as steel, concrete, brick, acoustic tiles, carpeting, padded seats, etc. The once mighty reverberant sound of the pipe organ is often almost entirely swallowed up in these new environments. Generally, little can be done about it.

Occasionally, even the organist admits to being frustrated with common quirks inherent in pipe organs. For instance, the variation in tuning as a function of temperature, humidity, and barometric pressure is well known. Sometimes a pipe organ is rendered unplayable because it's so far out of tune. More often, everyone just tolerates it. Pipe organs are massive, mechanical machines subject to various failure mechanisms. Wooden parts sensitive to variation in humidity become warped, cracked, and jammed. Critical leather parts deteriorate and fail. Worn-out motors, blowers, bellows, and regulators are common. Pipes can be stuck "off" or, more seriously, they can be stuck "on" much to the chagrin of the organist.

Another very important factor must be addressed at this point. It has to do with who controls the fate of the organ as a musical instrument. On one hand, we have the "elitists" who believe they alone have the expertise to determine what is proper in the world of organs. On the other hand, we have the "ordinary people" who do most of the listening and are often the ones paying the bills. In the middle are the organ designers and manufacturers without whom the organ would be just a mind exercise. Finally, and perhaps most crucial to the future of the organ, we have the "realists" who seek to achieve the best balance between traditional values and the realities of today's world.

The realist viewpoint is reflected in the following quote from a university professor of music who had just critiqued a recent Allen installation and wrote to me with his findings:

"I find no difference between the sound of the Allen and any of the many piped instruments I have played in the past forty years. Indeed the sound quality of the Allen exceeds many of those wind-blown instruments.

I can imagine places and situations in which, for historical or aesthetic reasons, a wind-blown pipe organ would be necessary. However, for most practical church and institutional installations, the electronic-blown (pipe) organ seems most desirable."

In contrast, the elitists appear to be more concerned with the form of the organ than its overall utility. They are often the most vocal and aggressive in pushing their views. Because of their persistent activism in trying to control the direction of organ development, it would be well to understand more deeply the nature of the elitist influence.

In the following paragraphs I will go into a little more detail about the evolution of the pipe organ with respect to the elitists—their attempt to control the details of pipe organ construction according to their own parochial viewpoint and their lack of regard for the overall success and acceptance of the instrument. I will then reference a recent, well-documented, real-life example of a hotly-contested, yet very successful, Allen installation.

First, let me share with you recollections of one personal encounter I had with elitists in France in the spring of 1980. A new Allen Organ was being dedicated and I had made arrangements to attend. As I approached the church, I saw people handing out leaflets. As I took one, I realized that these folks were actually protesting the installation of the organ. The following, which has been translated accurately, to the best of my knowledge, from the original French, is excerpted from their handout. Sadly, the local organist became part of the emotional protest and refused to play the organ. Thus, the church was forced to let the organist go. In turn, this incident was used by the elitist protesters as a further "call to arms." In the end, cooler heads prevailed, and the organ was well received by the "ordinary people" of the congregation.

> The acquisition of the "Allen" Electronic Organ has stirred lively controversy among organists and musicians of St. ...* Church.
>
> In effect, this instrument is an organ in name only.
>
> In a region like ..., which one could legitimately call a "land of organs," in a church like St. ..., which has known a prestigious musical past, it is inadmissible that one should cause to come from America a mass-produced instrument.

We possess world-renowned organbuilders who would have been able to realize a quite superior instrument at the same price (around 200,000 Fr.), and which would have been a true organ endowed with its proper qualities and of a personality that one would not abandon....

Let us recall that, according to the directives from the Second Vatican Council, the Church recognizes only the pipe organ as the true instrument suitable to perform liturgical functions...WHERE ARE THE PIPES IN THE ELECTRONIC "ALLEN" ORGAN OF...

Know equally that for taking a position against the acquisition of this "Allen electronic organ," and for wishing for St. ... Church an organ worthy of the name, Mr. ..., after 23 years of devotion to the parish, has seen himself notified of dismissal by the...Council.

* Names of persons and places purposely deleted.

Recent debate among pipe organ enthusiasts has revolved around the mechanics immediately behind the keys of the organ. The pipe organs of the Middle Ages and on into the 1800s were entirely mechanical. The keys on these organs were connected directly to the valves by means of mechanical linkages. As a result, the name "tracker" or "mechanical" organs evolved.

During the late 1800s, with the advent of electricity, organ builders who sought to improve their designs turned to electromagnetic keying systems. With this system, the depression of keys caused the closure of electrical contacts. The contacts acted as switches relating to the turning on and off of electromagnets which, in turn, physically opened and closed the valves. Use of electromagnetic keying allowed the console to be easily moved away from the sound generation part of the organ to a more appropriate location.

With electromagnetic keying in place and electric-motor-driven wind supplies, organ designers realized that they were no longer restricted to a low pressure system—the air pressure could be increased without affecting playability. In turn, increased air pressure allowed changing the tonal characteristics of the organ either for the better or for the worse depending on one's listening taste or intellectual bias. The application of electricity to the art of pipe organ building resulted in organs with their own distinctive sound and "feel." These are generally referred to as electropneumatic organs.

After World War II, there was a revival of the tracker organ among the elitists. It is not certain why this happened. Perhaps the great movement of troops into Europe during the War brought some American organists into contact with the old European tracker organs. These organists would have been used to the electropneumatic organs which predominated in America during the early and mid-1900s. The European trackers with their more intimate sound and playing "feel" would have contrasted sharply with the fuller, more romantic sound of the electropneumatics. Perhaps enough of these organists were captivated by the tracker that they sparked the renaissance or reinterest in the mechanical action organ, a renaissance which has now been ongoing for the last few decades.

The problem with this great swing backwards is that the elitists attempt to control the world of pipe organs including the design details of new installations. They often convince the "ordinary people" that a tracker organ is the only kind acceptable. After the tracker is installed, the elitist organists may be happy playing it. However, the "ordinary people," perhaps intuitively expecting to hear the more popular, romantic sound of the earlier electropneumatics, are not always able to comprehend the organist's enthusiasm for the tracker and end up losing interest in listening to the organ. Extending this scenario many times, I fear that, unless the interests of the "ordinary people" in the audience are taken into consideration by those making the decisions about new organ installations, the fate of the organ as a musical instrument may be placed in grave jeopardy.

So far I have been talking about pipe organs. What does all that have to do with Allen Digital Computer Organs? Well, Allens are outselling pipe organs by an overwhelming margin. Given the success we have had in building high quality organs, it is entirely possible that the Allen Digital Computer Organ will become the next major step in the long evolution of the organ as a viable musical instrument. In spite of our success, or perhaps because of it, the Allen Digital Computer

Organ, with its ability to faithfully capture the nuances of pipe organ sound be they low pressure or high pressure, is perceived by the elitists as a threat to the pipe organ. So, by the 1980s, the elitists closed ranks in hopes of preventing this "outsider" from penetrating what they consider to be a sacred bastion and the sole preserve of the pipe organ. Exhibiting the same stubbornness they showed in swinging so many pipe organ decisions towards trackers, they loudly proclaimed that they already "knew" what was "correct" about organ building without further examination and summarily dismissed the Allen as well as all the technology behind it.

Sometimes the tactics of the elitists take on the vehemence of a holy war. Such was the case with the recent purchase of an Allen Digital Computer Organ by Michigan State University in East Lansing, Michigan. Much of the story was documented by the local newspaper, the Lansing *State Journal*. Various articles including pro and con arguments appeared several months before we delivered and installed the completed organ.

The following article appeared on October 24, 1988, after the organ had been taken through its paces in several concerts.

Today   Lansing State Journal • Monday, Oct. 24, 1988

Jury in on Wharton organ: Wonderful

By KEN GLICKMAN
Lansing State Journal

REVIEW

In the past several weeks, we have had the opportunity to hear Wharton Center's brand new Allen Digital Organ in several different settings. But concerts Saturday and Sunday were the real test.

Internationally famous organ soloist Berj Zamkochian was in town for a pair of concerts that would surely show off the organ to its fullest potential.

Most people were withholding judgment until they heard the instrument in the hands of a true artist playing major organ works.

The opinions of the audiences at these concerts were unanimously positive. Takis Pizanis, local pianist, organist and conductor, said, "I think it's wonderful. It passes with flying colors."

James Niblock, retired chair of the Michigan State School of Music, said, "If you closed your eyes, it almost sounded like a French Cathedral organ."

These enthusiastic comments were given after a stunning concert with Zamkochian and the Michigan State University Symphony Orchestra, with Leon Gregorian conducting. They performed the three standards works for orchestra and organ: the concerto by Poulenc and the organ symphonies by Copland and Saint-Saens.

Zamkochian proved to the packed Wharton audience why he was organist with the Boston Symphony for so many years. He is a musician who truly plays the organ as simply another instrument with the orchestra, blending effortlessly in tutti passages and rising to the role of soloist when called for.

His consistent sense of musical phrasing made this huge instrument sound supple and agile. his technique in the vivacious Copland was impressive,

and his sense of the dramatic was brought to the fore in the Saint-Saens.

But Zamkochian's artistic playing would have been lost if the instrument or the orchestra were not up to par. The new organ sounded magnificent, and the orchestra was precise and lyrical. This ensemble has made great strides in the last several years.

On Sunday, Zamkochian had Wharton to himself. In a solo recital, he played three major works by Bach, plus other pieces which put the new instrument through its paces. William McHarris, physics professor, composer and organist said, "I love it. I honestly think that people who didn't know it wasn't a pipe organ would think that it was."

Visiting Wharton for this special dedication concert was a group of professional organists from Fort Wayne, Ind. Ira Gerig said "It's definitely a state-of-the-art digital organ. It actually produces pipe sounds."

Vincent Stater of Fort Wayne said, "The major criteria is not if it's pipe or not. Rather, is it a fine musical instrument? This is." He also said that the Wharton Instrument is a bit too heavy, that it overfills the hall.

That opinion was shared by Ken Stein, also from Fort Wayne, who said that it was better to hear this organ from the back of the hall as it takes some of the edge off the sound. He also commented that that problem could be adjusted rather easily.

Rae Chin of Lansing said: "For the programs produced in this facility, this has the most useful voices and blend for

(continued on next page)

ensemble and solo work. It sounds just like a pipe organ. I could feel the pipes."

The jury has been out on the organ—but after this weekend it is back, and the verdict is clear. The new electronic organ sounds good, sounds loud and, if you close your eyes, sounds like a pipe organ.

Mission completed and successful.*

In this chapter I have reviewed some of the realities challenging the practicality of the pipe organ in today's world. As previously stated, the elitists are having a difficult time adjusting to these realities and, in my view, are too enraptured with the glories of the past to accurately perceive the present and future. In their zeal to move backwards, they have often given poor advice, which has resulted in many costly "sacrificial offerings" to the "pipe organ goddess."

I do not mean to overly chastise the elitists, but rather I want to awaken the "ordinary people" to the very real pitfalls into which they are often lured. I challenge the realists among the organ enthusiasts to resist the ever-present peer pressure and express their viewpoint to those making decisions concerning new organ installations. Finally, I suggest that those making these decisions give top priority to the quality of the organ "sound" and the overall "musical" success of the instrument.

Some of my encounters with the establishment have the makings of a good fairy tale. The following "tongue-in-cheek story" is based on <u>actual events</u> surrounding a proposed organ installation, and I hope, will serve to further illustrate the influence presently

*Format changed for legibility

enjoyed by the elitists. The names have been changed, of course, to protect privacy.

✳ ✳ ✳ ✳ ✳

There once was a kingdom called Org. The inhabitants of Org revered the pipe organ. Although there were many pipe organs installed throughout the land, the people could not afford to install too many new pipe organs because they were becoming so very expensive. The pipe organ builders of Org were sad. If they couldn't sell many new pipe organs, their children would grow hungry. In desperation, some of them ventured to far off lands, such as the U.S.A., to sell their beloved pipes. They found that many of these foreigners also had learned to revere pipe organs, and some were even willing to buy new ones—new pipe organs built by the Organians. This made the pipe organ builders of Org happy.

One day a wandering organist visited Org. He brought with him a new kind of organ, an Allen Digital Computer Organ, which he planned to play in concert. This was very risky. He knew that Org's high priests of pipe organ reverence would be very angry indeed. They would say that the Allen Organ was a false organ and should be banished from Org before unspeakable misfortunes befell the entire kingdom. But the wandering organist was very brave. He did not fear the high priests. However, he was worried about the high priestess, Madame Aspingrass. Her influence was legendary. The wandering organist was not totally alone, though. The Prince of Org was his friend, and the organist knew that the Prince would be able to protect the musician from serious harm.

The Prince was very wise. He knew about organs and was even an organist himself. The Allen Organ intrigued him. He knew that the Allen was based on modern technology, and he was concerned that the kingdom of Org would fall far behind the times if it closed its doors to new ideas. However, he also knew that he was Prince to all the people of Org, even those who refused to open their minds to the new ideas.

By and by the wandering organist, with the blessings of the Prince, set up the Allen Organ in a suitable place and the daring concert was announced. The kingdom was buzzing with anticipation. On the night of the concert, some prominent residents of the kingdom were in attendance. As the concert progressed, the audience became more and more awed with the great quality and diversity of the performance. Many even forgot that they were not supposed to enjoy the sounds coming from this "false" organ and succumbed to enchantment. After the concert they realized what happened and were confused. If the Allen Organ is so bad, why does it sound so good? Some didn't know what to believe and were afraid. Some believed what they heard, and they knew what they heard was good.

One man, the Duke of Clearthought, was very impressed with what he saw (and heard) at the concert and had a vision. He wanted Org to be part of what he believed was a revolution in the art of organ building. He wanted Org to commission the Allen Organ Company to build one of the finest organs devised by man. The Prince was delighted with the plan and gave his support to the project. A famous organist/designer from the U.S.A. would act as a consultant.

The Duke contacted Allen Organ Company in far-off America. After preliminary discussions, the Duke asked Allen's president, Jerome Markowitz, to come to Org for further discussions at the proposed site of the installation. Jerome agreed and plans were made for the trip.

At the appointed hour, Jerome and his wife, Martha, left their home in Allentown, and they set out for the far-away kingdom of Org. When they arrived at the airport in Org, they looked all around. The Duke had told them that someone would pick them up at the airport and take them to a hotel. When they found their escort, they realized that they were going to be taken to the finest hotel in Org. And, they would be travelling there in a royal limousine. They were very impressed. They sensed that their visit to Org was going to be very different from life back home in Allentown.

Jerome and Martha received royal treatment while in this kingdom of Org. There was a pipe organ concert, of course, attended by the Prince and other royal dignitaries. There was the invitation to the Royal Palace for lunch with the Prince and other luminaries associated with the Allen Organ project. These affairs were punctuated with all of the pomp and impeccable elegance of the royal presence. Jerome and Martha were dazzled by this glimpse of royal life in Org, but Jerome sensed that, in some circles, there was an uneasiness over his visit to this land of the pipe organ.

After discussions and acoustic tests at the proposed installation site, Jerome was sure that Allen Organ Company could build a very fine organ for the kingdom of Org, one that would meet all the high expectations of those backing the project. On the surface, all appeared to be in order for proceeding with the grand design. Jerome and Martha bid farewell to their new found friends from Org and headed home.

Back in Org, as word of the Allen Organ project spread throughout the land, Madame Aspingrass and the high priests of pipe organ reverence grew more and more livid. This ominous threat to the sanctity of Org's pipe organ establishment had to be squashed quickly. Retaliation was swift. The Prince was informed that, unless the Allen Organ project was stopped, disruptive actions would be taken throughout the land. The Prince, concerned for the general welfare of the kingdom, regretfully withdrew his support for the project. On this occasion, Madame Aspingrass and her fellow protectors of the pipes would have their way. The people of Org would have to wait until another day for their Allen Digital Computer Organ.

"10,000" Organ Designers

The pipe organ consists of ranks of pipes which are controlled by means of stops, keys, and pedals. Each rank of pipes has its own tone color, its own stop, and its own name, which is written on the stop. If a particular stop is pulled out, the various pipes within the corresponding rank can be played by means of the keys or pedals. A small organ may be equipped with as few as two or three ranks. A large organ may be equipped with several hundred. Each pipe is said to speak with a certain distinctive "voice," the characteristics of which are controlled by the mechanical design and adjustment of the pipe. Over the centuries, organ builders have devised a whole spectrum of voices. To a large extent, the quality of an organ depends on the aesthetic quality of each individual voice and how well the various voices of the organ blend together. There are an infinite number of possible variations in the design or "specification" of a given organ. Allen Organs, which emulate pipe organs, exhibit this same versatility. The situation can be likened to that of an artist selecting individual colors and combinations of colors for a work of art. The variations are endless. Some choices turn out to be aesthetically quite successful. And, of course, some choices turn out to be rather ugly.

If we look at the broader world of musical instrument building, we see that it is unusual to have so many options in the construction of a given instrument. For example, a piano has only one "voice," and that one voice cannot deviate very much from the expected "piano sound" before we are reluctant to accept it as a true piano. I don't mean to minimize the task of the piano builder. Certainly, there are tremendous qualitative and tonal factors to be considered by the piano specialist. However, the target at which the piano builder is aiming is more sharply defined than in the case of the organ builder. As a result, it is rare to find a pianist who is deeply "into" the design and mechanics of the piano. Such matters are generally left to the acknowledged experts, the piano builders, and technicians. In contrast, because of manifold variations from organ to organ, musicians and other organ enthusiasts must, of necessity, study and develop a certain understanding of the many different arrangements of the ranks of pipes in organs. Thus has been spawned an army of organ "experts" who are eager to tell the organ builder how to build the world's greatest instrument.

In many cases when an organ is purchased, an organist or other key music specialist will insist upon some arrangement of ranks and stops which the organ builder knows is far from typical and may even be unique. Pity the poor organ builder in this situation. He has devoted his life to the problems of organ construction, and has seen his share of "bright ideas" turn into white elephants. His practical experience often puts him at odds with the more exotic views of the customer. Should he speak up and risk creating a personal gulf between himself and the customer or should he simply assume a laissez-faire posture?

As a vintage organ builder, I have had my share of well-meaning, yet off-the-wall, "bright ideas" with which to deal. I'm not sure I've run into all "10,000" organ designers out there but certainly a good number of them. I'm not one to look the other way when I sense a white elephant in the making. Accordingly, I've always expressed my views, albeit as gingerly as possible, usually with good results. Admittedly, however, there are a few organs here and there which have slipped out with some features which, in my opinion, border on the harebrained. These are monuments to those would-be organ "experts" who, in spite of diligent warnings, have insisted on "having their own way."

Friendly
& Unfriendly
People

Early on, I had hoped that organ building would be an island in the stormy seas of the business world. I thought that building organs would be a particularly peaceful endeavor bringing me into contact with only the friendliest of people. Now, after having a half century or so to reflect on this early dream, I must confess that my youthful vision was somewhat naive. For along with the many wonderful friends and acquaintances which I did indeed gather over the years, Allen Organ Company and I seem to have snagged our share of misanthropes. At first, this gave me cause for concern, but I later realized that, in the great scheme of things, if we live our lives fully, we must inevitably deal with both friend and foe alike. Let me elaborate.

Few organ people view the business of organ building impassively. Happily, the vast majority of people I've encountered over the years as an organ builder have responded quite positively to the work going on at Allen. Pipe organ "elitists" are, of course, a glaring exception.

Another kind of "Allen Organ basher" turns up from time to time—the local "techno-guru." These individuals often have enough of a technical background to command respect from the local following. Sometimes we inadvertently become food for their mischievous appetite. Without warning, "techno-gurus" can become pesky "techno-bullies" or "techno-hecklers." Perhaps we somehow rubbed them the wrong way. Maybe they're jealous of our technical accomplishments. Maybe they consider it just a sport. Whatever the reason for their behavior, the "techno-bully-hecklers" can certainly try one's patience. It seems that no amount of scientific explanation will curb their barbs. And, given the esoteric nature of organ technicalities, the "techno-guru" can sometimes maintain a firm grip on the sentiments of a local following. Getting a fair trial under these conditions is not easy. Sometimes we can't even get into the courtroom.

One example—a chap in England wrote us a letter in the mid-1970s taking issue with our claim that the heart of our new digital organ was, in essence, a computer. We responded, in defense, with all of the technical dialog and dissertation which such a "weighty" matter commands. Apparently he did not like our explanation. Ever since that encounter, he has gone out of his way to bad mouth our products whenever the opportunity presents itself.

I suppose, in a sense, we are dealing with one of those quirks of human nature with which, I'm sure, we all encounter from time to time—the dogged avoidance of having to say, "I was wrong." I know of at least one "techno-bully" who expended a great deal of energy taking a "position" about supposed "technical flaws" in the "Allen-engineered" organ. Apparently, he finally reached a point where he could no longer deny our technical arguments. However, rather than simply say, "I was wrong," he chose instead to endorse an allegedly similar organ—similar but one produced by an Allen competitor.

Fortunately for Allen, such tenacious gadflies are in the minority. Sometimes, when we do encounter a pesky backbiter, he or she can be sent away with a quick shrug of the shoulder. Otherwise, we just say to ourselves, "C'est la vie."

Competition

Under our free enterprise system, companies compete with one another for the customers' purchases. This competition manifests itself in many different ways. Some companies invest in research and development to come up with attractive new products. Some companies "clone" the successful products of others. Some companies try to build a good reputation with customers through years of stability and service. Some companies lure customers by claiming everything under the sun in their advertising, whether true or not. No individual company can afford to ignore the actions taken by all the other companies in its market. Whether we like it or not, the history of each company is inextricably intertwined with that of its competitors.

Competition is certainly not new to the organ business. For example, the famous "Battle of the Organs" took place in England in the latter 1600s. Bernard

Smith and Renatus Harris were prominent pipe organ builders in competition with each other at that time. Both men sought the contract to build an organ for the Temple Church in London. After much haggling, a decision was made to allow both men to build organs at different locations in the church. A public trial of the instruments was to decide which would stay and which would go.

The "Battle," which took several years to run its course, must have placed an enormous financial strain on both organ builders. According to rumor, with so much at stake, one builder even tried to sabotage his competitor's instrument. In the end, both organs were deemed to be excellent. However, Smith was given the nod, and Harris, much frustrated, had to remove his instrument.

A few centuries after the "Battle of the Organs," competition among organ builders was still going strong. In 1935, Hammond introduced the first commercially successful all-electric organ. The Hammond Organ, of course, became enormously popular. Early on, it was touted as being a competitor to the pipe organ. In reality, it didn't sound like a pipe organ at all. However, its sound had various other unique characteristics which became highly prized by many popular music performers throughout the world. In essence, the Hammond created its own market, essentially separate from the pipe organ market. So, for many years following its introduction, the Hammond Organ was a great commercial success, regardless of its limitations in competing with pipe organs.

By the time Allen Organ Company was getting off the ground, the Hammond Organ was so well established that it, in essence, became the standard of comparison for the other non-pipe organs to follow. Often, when a pioneer product such as the Hammond appears, competitors spring up looking for a piece of the action. In recent years, in the case of the personal computer, competitors have introduced products which are more or less indistinguishable from the pioneer product in functionality, but cost less. These successor products are aptly described as "clones." The early Allen Organs sounded much more like a pipe organ than a Hammond. So although we recognized the market potential in "cloning" the Hammond, we chose instead to further distance ourselves from the Hammond in hopes of creating our own market. The goal of Allen Organ Company was, at that time, to emulate the pipe organ as closely as possible. In fact, over the years, my guiding principle has been to make the Allen sound so much like a pipe organ as to be indistinguishable from it.

As Allen Organs "caught on" with those seeking the sound of pipes without the problems of pipes, competitors began to spring up in our market niche. In the late 1940s other companies introduced products which appeared to be aimed at this market. Examples include Baldwin, even at that time a long-established piano manufacturer; Conn, the famous band instrument producer; and Wurlitzer, well-known for its theater pipe organs. These companies, among others, followed Allen's lead rather than that of Hammond, who continued to produce their unique pioneering product in substantial quantities.

Between those early years and the present time, well over twenty different manufacturers appeared on the scene in an attempt to capitalize on our lead. In several cases, the appearance was only transitory. Getting started was easy, but keeping the business going was more difficult. The organ industry was such that it was possible, especially in the early years, to become a start-up manufacturer with relatively little capital. The newcomers didn't have much to lose. The main hurdle was learning the technology. In some cases, the start-up had actually received "training" by servicing Allen Organs.

I suppose having start-ups trying to emulate one's product is a good measure of one's success. At its best, this type of competition is also good for the customer. As the competitors spar for position, the better companies will be more eager to advance the state of the art. They will submit yet a better product to the test of the marketplace, where the ultimate judge is invariably the customer. However, competition isn't always at its best.

Several aspects of the organ business foster a temptation for some to employ more unsavory competitive techniques. For instance, organs are "big ticket" items. Accordingly, a competitor can't afford to lose too many individual sales. In this high pressure atmosphere, a competitor can sometimes go "way beyond" the boundaries of honest competition. Consider, for example, the following quote from the sales manual of one of Allen's competitors:

> Terrorizing is a full-time sport. You must enjoy doing a job on someone for maximum effect. Knowing how to do it also helps you recognize when a competitor is trying to terrorize you! It takes many months, sometimes years, to get to your competitors. However, unless you start right away, you will never enjoy the benefits of properly terrorized competitors.

> . Misinformation

> A variation of the rumor, which usually has a kernel of fact or is totally factual, is misinformation. Presented as a rumor to competitors it is designed to really put them in a spin. If they repeat it to customers, they will likely be looked upon as foolish because the idea will seem so outrageous. Examples might be telling them a smaller competitor is going out of business, that a key church they are competing in has decided to buy a tracker, or any other sort of crazy thing. These must be stated as rumor, not fact, and you must swear them to secrecy. Use them sparsely so they cannot tell the misinformation from actual rumors. It adds to the fun!

. Letters from Lawyers.

In some cases it may be appropriate to send a dealer
a letter from your lawyer threatening a lawsuit (even
if the grounds are shady) for libel or slander, just to
shake up their game. Most people will change their
tactics if they think they might get sued.

I expect the reader will have the same feeling that I
experienced when I first read the words quoted above.
Is this par for the ethical standards of the American
business community today? Why has a supposedly
legitimate business enterprise stooped to using such
deplorable methods? Well, for one reason, it's effective,
at least in the short run—like using poison gas in
warfare.

Tactics such as those described above exploit man's
trusting nature. I believe that people, by instinct, tend
to assume that information from a "friendly" source is
factual. If the "friendly" source happens to throw in
some "misinformation," the chances are good that it
will be accepted as fact. Thus, the company or dealer
using such tactics might first establish a "friendly"
rapport with the potential customer. If a competitor
appears on the scene, the "friendly" company or dealer
feeds the customer some disparaging "misinformation"
about the competing company or its product. More
often than not, the customer will then develop a
negative attitude towards the competing company, an
attitude that is difficult to turn around. The

unsuspecting customer can easily end up buying an inferior product from the "friendly" misinformer.

For an actual example of the use of "misinformation," consider the following quote from one of the "misinformation" letters used against Allen. The excerpt is from a recent letter written to a church pastor by one of Allen's competitors who was frustrated by the favorable reception Allen received from the organ search committee at the church.

> "I presume that you do know that The Allen Company has been for sale for many months now since the founder and major stockholder, Jerome Markowitz, is in the process of retirement and to the best of our knowledge at this point in time, no buyer is on the immediate horizon."

As plausible as this statement might sound, it was totally inaccurate. The letter also included various technical misstatements along with allusions to the "high degree of trust" established between the pastor and the author of the letter. Trust indeed!

Although we all accept that organ builders have to make a living selling their product, I believe that many people are loath to think about church organs the way they think about other more familiar products such as automobiles or soap powder. The church organ has always enjoyed a certain mystique all its own. To the average person, both pipe and electronic organs are mysterious entities fully understood by only a handful of specialists. In sharp contrast, there are millions of car buffs who can readily reel off the technical pros and cons of the various models. Arguments in support of or against a particular model car are often laced with technical jargon which is substantially well understood by the various proponents. However, organs are far less familiar. As a result, I suspect that those either purchasing an organ for their church or having one rebuilt will exercise less informed scrutiny than they would when, for example, they shop for the family automobile. They may tend to assume that suppliers of goods and services to religious institutions are somehow above a shady deal. In reality, churches have had their share of rip-offs. For example, I know of an extreme case recently where a pipe organ repairman disappeared with a large quantity of the church's money before doing his work. Regretfully, this has happened before. Other less obvious rip-offs occur all too often.

When members of a church or other institution are faced with the purchase of an organ, how do they obtain the information upon which to base their decisions? For one thing, they almost always call on the local "expert." This could be an organist who, if nothing else, knows a good deal more about organs than those charged with the selection decision. In such a situation, the advisor can easily command an inordinate amount of influence. The weakness in this situation is that the typical advisor may lean heavily towards one particular school of thought based on a very narrow viewpoint.

They may endow organs with an overly romantic or classic character, for example.

In defending personal ideals, the advisor may casually dismiss practical considerations. The advisor may even refuse to look at the organ as a machine which obeys the laws of nature. Relying too heavily on the local "expert" to provide direction increases the susceptibility to being misguided by overly aggressive competitors. For example, I've been told that it is common in some countries for a pipe organ company to provide the local organist/adviser with a tidy kickback on a sale of a product. Less direct cultivation techniques such as stroking an ego are more common. The "expert" might very well turn to a company who is the "friendliest" when it comes time to buy an organ. Prominent organists have even been allowed the use of an instrument on a "permanent loan" basis. The competitor using this ploy typically suggests that the organist "chose" the competitor's product over everyone else's purely on the basis of merit. Given the complexity of today's organ technology, opportunities abound to cover up deficiencies or paint exaggerated images. The local "expert" can easily be swayed by tricky rhetoric or well-orchestrated demonstrations. It's a rare purchaser who will even insist on examining the inside of the console in order to check for quality of construction.

Another manifestation of competition is the need to know what market to go after. For example, at one time the home or popular organ market was booming.

Various organ companies aimed a great deal of their engineering development efforts at new products for this market at the expense of their institutional product line. Perhaps the fast buck was a factor. The predominant quest was for more and more sophisticated "easy-play" features. Tonal quality was given far less attention than the flashy control panels which were all too characteristic of the home organ of the 1970s. Early on we saw the appearance of automatic rhythm systems. Press a button, and rhythm accompaniment would spontaneously commence!

Other automatic features were developed to take over more of the playing. Chordal accompaniment became available. By the late 1970s an owner of an "easy-play" organ merely had to play a solo sequence with one finger, and various types of rhythm and chordal accompaniments would "follow."

But easy-play organs carried the seeds of their own destruction. Invariably, owners found that easy play could only provide transitory satisfaction. The initial novelty didn't last long. The realization gradually set in that an easy play organ was suspiciously akin to a much less costly record player or cassette deck. Customer attitude toward the easy-play home organ turned toward the negative almost overnight. By the 1980s, the financial strain caused by diminishing sales took its toll on the industry. In this case, the pressures of competition resulted in strategies which benefited neither the customer nor the competitors who adopted these strategies. I'm thankful I resisted the lure of the easy-play era and kept Allen Organ out of it.

Also, at times, the church or institutional organ market has been sensitive to what appears to be the "latest and greatest" technology. I have occasionally seen churches literally leap into a deal based on the promise of an unproven technological "breakthrough" by a relative newcomer to the church organ business. In our high-tech world, some customers don't want to be caught with what might be construed as yesterday's technology. Competitors are very much aware of this consciousness of technology in the marketplace and, accordingly, are constantly offering the technological "wave of the future." I've seen an endless stream of these "breakthroughs" appear on the market over the years. Some succeed, but most fail. How can organ purchasers accurately evaluate apparent breakthroughs in technology? There is no easy answer to this question. Perhaps common sense is still the best guide. Does the organ actually sound better than the alternatives? Does it appear to be well built? Are other purchasers satisfied? What about the company's business record over the years and their general reputation for customer support, service, quality of construction, etc.?

Of course, the problem of evaluating the viability of new developments in technology is not new. For example, in the 1950s and 1960s we saw breakthroughs based on tone waveforms photographically replicated onto various kinds of spinning disks. Readout of the tone waveforms was done by a non-contacting pickup, such as photoelectric or capacitive. I believe a gentleman by the name of Ivan Eremeeff devised one of the first systems of this type in the 1930s. Compton, in England, actually built many such instruments in that same time frame. Electrovoice later introduced a photoelectric version of the system.

I recall a church, in the early 1960s, that was in the market for a new organ. The church was faced with deciding between competing technologies. Electrovoice came in with their promising new photoelectric disk technology while we offered our well-established oscillator system. Allen was rejected over the Electrovoice spinning disk organ because a technically oriented member of the church was convinced that the photoelectric disk technology was, without a doubt, the wave of the future. To him, playing back the sounds of *actual recorded pipes* logically had to be *more like pipes* than the sound of Allen's electronic oscillators. Subsequently, the disk organ was installed in the church, but it quickly exhibited insurmountable operational problems. Fortunately, the church was able to back out of the purchase within a month or two and ended up buying an Allen after all. Eventually the spinning disk organ was discontinued, apparently because of continued operational difficulties. Even seemingly well-founded ideas often defy operational reality.

My comments on competition and organ technology would not be complete without mention of the hybrid organ. As many an organ enthusiast knows, the costs associated with buying and maintaining a pipe organ have gone through the roof. In contrast, digital computer organs offer an attractive alternative—about a five-to-one cost and space advantage over a comparable pipe organ. Yet, in spite of the fact that the human ear has difficulty in distinguishing between an Allen and a similarly registered pipe organ, there are those who still cling to pipes. If they can't afford a complete pipe organ, they may opt for an incomplete pipe organ—as long as there are some pipes used somewhere. Thus, was born the hybrid organ; this was a combination of a pipe organ and an electronic organ— a would-be carnival merchant's dream product.

In some cases, Allens have been used in combination with pipes. However, I've always discouraged this kind of arrangement. To begin with, aside from pipes being expensive and very difficult to work with, the tuning of the entire organ will be dictated by the pipes which are sensitive to temperature, to humidity, and to barometric pressure. The tuning stability and flexibility of the digital computer organ used in combination with these pipes can't be effectively utilized in this situation. Furthermore, pipes and pipe organs are esoteric machines and require a high level of knowledge and experience to manipulate them. Digital Computer Organs are conceptually different from pipe organs. Therefore, repairs on a hybrid organ will require the services of entirely different personnel for each of these entities. All in all, I feel that the money spent on the pipe voices of a hybrid organ would be better spent on additional Allen voices.

More than one organ company has taken advantage of the misguided affinity for pipes often found in some congregations by promoting the hybrid organ as the ideal organ. The hybrid organ appears, on the surface, to satisfy both the pipe organ holdouts and those responsible for the budget. The salesman will call it the best of both worlds. However, I see it as the worst of both worlds.

As far as Allen Organ is concerned, I have tried to meet the competition with a balance of new technology combined with scrupulous advertising and reasonable sales tactics, conscientious after-sale support, and proven records of service. For example, if we compare the Allen Digital Computer Organ of today with one made in the 1970s, we do indeed see and hear differences. We have made steady technological improvements over the years, but only when and where we believe our customers will benefit. This conservative approach may have lost some individual sales. However, I remain convinced, after more than fifty years in the business, that my approach to the pressures of competition is, in the final analysis, the best one.

Adventures
at Sea

Being a restless experimenter, I've undertaken a few projects which ran into some bad weather in the marketplace. In each of these cases, I was completely confident that the project would sail smoothly on a sea of friendly acceptance and sublime success. Like an adventurous mariner excitedly setting sail in a craft of his own making, I believed my new boat would meet only the gentlest wave and calmest breeze. In spite of my resolute confidence in the soundness of my new idea, I was, at times, rudely reminded that the marketplace, as with the sea, can turn stormy, whether we're sailing on it or not. On these particular occasions, as I found myself being tossed unceremoniously into the cold water, I was thankful that I had long ago learned how to swim. Let me present a few examples.

By the early 1940s, events in Europe led to concern in this country for self-preservation in the event of war.

I recall reading and hearing about the possibility of our having to deal with air raids. One of the most prominent aspects of dealing with an air raid was the use of the conventional, motor-driven siren devices used to warn the people to find shelter. Well, I thought I had come up with a better solution to the problem of building and deploying sirens all over the country—the Allen Siren.

I had discovered that I could modify the circuitry of an Allen Organ oscillator so that the output tone would "wail"—just like sirens are supposed to "wail." By amplifying this tone and using a public-address type of speaker arrangement I managed to produce a "wailing"

The Allen Siren—early 1940s

sound of ear-splitting intensity. I visualized a grateful reception by the "authorities" when I offered them my siren idea. Instead I received a "thanks, but no thanks" reply, thus ending that particular adventure.

During the 1960s, we were looking for more penetration of the home market. In trying to come up with new products for this market I thought I had hit on a "sure" winner. As I let my mind drift about searching for something that would be appealing to me if I were the customer, I thought about the circus. I vividly remembered seeing the spectacular pageantry, smelling the aroma of fresh popcorn, and hearing the circus organ—the calliope. Yes! The calliope! Of course! A miniature electronic calliope had to be a "sure" winner—and it was certainly organ-related. I thought that almost everyone would surely want their own calliope. My calliope idea was molded into what looked like an excellent product. It sounded like a calliope; it played like a calliope; it even looked somewhat like a calliope. Yet, it was small enough to be rolled out of the way into a corner, serving then as decoration and conversation piece, until its owner once again had that overwhelming urge to play his or her circus organ, at which time it could simply be wheeled out ready to rekindle recollections of those wonderful magic moments at the circus.

When we announced our calliope and presented it to the market, I was stunned by how few calliope players there really are in this world. What I envisioned as a marketing splash amounted only to a marketing spatter. What a disappointment! I am consoled, however, by a very small but loyal cadre of calliope enthusiasts who have the same fondness for the calliope as I do— enthusiasts who still, to this day, call or write about either obtaining parts for their vintage instruments or obtaining a whole new calliope—actually hoping that we still manufacture them.

Again in the "smashing" new product category, in the late 1960s, we had the Allen "Carousel." The Carousel was a "one-man-band"—a musician's dream. It had all sorts of instruments ready to be called into play at the flick of a stop—mandolins, piano, banjo, balalaika, zither, guitar, and sleigh bells, to name just a few. It even included one of my patented inventions, "flying hammers." The flying hammer idea was sparked by a gift I received from my wife, Martha. She had come across an obsolete, zither-type, acoustic instrument called a Marxaphone and gave it to me as a gift. It was equipped with a mechanical, repeating-type striking mechanism for each string. As I studied the unusual striking mechanism on this instrument, I thought I might be able to build something that would perform a similar function in an organ.

After experimenting with different arrangements, I finally perfected what I called "flying hammers." Those keys of the organ equipped with flying hammers were fitted with a spring metal contact onto the end of which was attached a metal weight. When the key was snapped down, the weighted spring contact would vibrate so as to make and break the electrical connection, which turned the tone generator on and off repetitiously. The overall effect sounded remarkably like the "tremolo" of a mandolin player.

Although "I" thoroughly enjoyed the sounds that could be created with the Carousel line of instruments and was convinced that we had a real winner, the Carousel did not sail especially well in the marketplace. In the end, I would have to call it just another adventure at sea. Nevertheless, as in the case of the calliope adventure, there are still a few Carousel purchasers who insist that their particular instrument is one of the greatest we ever built for home entertainment. Yet, in spite of the satisfaction I got from pleasing these few happy customers, these new-product adventures remind me of the wisdom of the often-heard, but less-practiced, business adage—that to be a broad commercial success, a product must suit the needs of the broad commercial marketplace rather than reflect only the parochial enthusiasm of its designer.

Then there was my simple solution to the problem of bombs being either taken or placed secretly on board commercial aircraft for evil purposes. Years ago, such bombs were occasionally used by people to hijack planes. Today, we are also faced with terrorists who use bombs for more sinister reasons. Because of my experience with radio transmitters and the like, I knew that energy can be transmitted through space and transformed into heat at a distant location. This fact, in my mind, was clearly the key to building a foolproof "bomb detector." I visualized a procedure by which the items to be checked for bombs would be placed into a remote shed where they would be exposed to a suitably powerful energy beam. I reasoned that all bombs require a detonator which would easily be detonated by exposure to the beam.

On February 2, 1960, I wrote this letter to the government agency in charge of such matters revealing my "clear" solution to the problem.

> I offer the following suggestion as a possible remedy for the bomb threats (and perhaps actual bombings) with which commercial aviation is now being afflicted.
>
> I recommend that a "shed" be installed on every ramp somewhere between the airline terminal and the location of the plane that is being loaded. This shed would be equipped with an electronic detonator. There are many devices which could be applied for this purpose, such as a pulse of radar or infra-red heat. It might be advisable to separate the baggage so that it can be pushed or conveyed through the detonator's focus. It would also be practical for the passengers to walk through this area, one at a time. Naturally an explosion will result if anyone has an explosive in their luggage. If this were to happen just once, this situation would certainly never re-occur.

By publicizing the system in newsreel (with an actual demonstration) and the wire services, it is probable that a bomb situation would never again present itself and, of course, telephone threats could be ignored.

If I can be of service in offering further explanation of such a device, do not hesitate to contact me.

I received no response to my letter and wondered whether my idea was considered harebrained.

As bomb threats increased in the 1980s, I once again, as recently as February 20, 1989, reminded the authorities about my "clear" solution by means of the following letter.

I note with interest that the FAA and also counterparts in foreign governments are wrestling with the problem of what to do about preventing future situations which might replicate the happenings of Pan Am Flight 103.

Enclosed is a copy of a letter that I wrote to the FAA in *February 1960*. The relevant technology existed then and, of course, most certainly exists now. Admittedly, there are numerous negative ramifications to such a plan. Yet, it does not appear that any alternative has yet been devised.

I am sure that I can speak for the millions of citizens who are hoping for a means of preventing another "Pan Am Flight 103."

Although I did, this time, receive a response by letter signed by The Secretary of Transportation, it amounted to a polite "No thank you." My "bomb detector" did not sail well at all, yet I would love to see some other adventurous mariner conquer this bombing plague.

Epilogue

I have always been deeply impressed by the sound of a good pipe organ and have constantly worked to make the Allen Organ sound as nearly like a pipe organ as possible. Now that the sound of the Allen is hardly distinguishable from that of a comparable pipe organ, I am compelled to address a much more profound issue. Can Allen now build a better organ than any pipe organ builder. Because of my own great respect for the pipe organ and given all the effort it took over several decades just to match its sound, I have never—until now—put myself in a position to face this question head on.

Carefully considering the most recent advances in Allen's technology, I have come to believe that today Allen can indeed build a better sounding organ than any pipe organ builder. I do not make this claim lightly, nor do I mean to denigrate the skills of pipe organ builders. The real issue is technology—as applied to tone production. Artisans have squeezed every last drop of musical capability out of the air-driven-pipe tone generator technology. Continuing to use air-driven-pipe technology to advance the art of organ building is futile. In sharp contrast, the Allen system offers an exciting future to organ artisans. The present Allen tone producing technology is already superior to anything possible with the air-driven-pipe technology. Therefore, I predict that in the not-too-distant future the pipe organ will be honored mainly as an artifact. The organ of the future will be much more like those being built by Allen today. Carrying this theme still farther, we might even speculate that a future generation might casually refer to their church organ as an Allen digital "pipe organ" in much the same way that we of this generation casually talk about a "steamroller" or a "steam shovel" knowing full well that these machines are no longer driven by steam but rather by diesel or gasoline engines.

To quote Shakespeare, "What's past is prologue...". As a result of our past efforts, Allen Organ Company, today, commands a dominant, worldwide position in the field of non-pipe organs. I have been especially pleased by the acceptance of our products overseas. The effort involved has been spearheaded by my son, Steven, in his position as Vice President of International Sales. I believe it is vitally important for us to understand and be an active part of today's changing world; much of our future markets lie overseas.

Perhaps because Western Europe was the area in which pipe organs were most highly developed over the centuries, a stronger interest in organs continues there as compared to the U.S.A. Organ recitals appear to be better attended and occur with more frequency. Hundreds of Allen Organs have been installed in each of the following countries: Great Britain, France, West Germany, and Switzerland. Scores of them have been purchased in all of the Scandinavian countries, except Denmark. Italy is an example of a country where we have not yet achieved a strong dealer organization. Yet, our organs have appeared there in prominent places through word-of-mouth endorsements.

One example of such an endorsement occurred a few years ago. Through the recommendation of my friend, Bishop Joseph McShea of the Allentown Diocese of the Roman Catholic Church, an Allen Organ was purchased for use in the Sistine Choir Concert Hall in Vatican City, Rome. Bishop McShea was quite familiar with Allen Organs having formerly presided over the St. Catharine of Siena Cathedral in Allentown, the site of an Allen Digital Computer Organ and, decades before, the site of the very first Allen Organ ever built and sold.

After word of the success of the Sistine Choir Concert Hall installation spread, other installations soon followed in the Accademia Santa Cecilia and, more recently, in Our Lady of All Graces Convent in Rome.

In 1986, because of the interest generated by the first two of the above instruments, an Allen Organ was purchased by the Precious Blood Parish Church in Florence, Italy. Soon after, interest apparently was fanned among some members of the congregation who were affiliated with the Teatro Comunale, the main opera house and concert hall in Florence. In 1988, a large three-manual Allen was installed in this establishment. We anticipate that this trend will continue.

Japan is a country which has no "organ culture" of its own. Yet, in recent years, the Japanese have developed a substantial interest in the classical organ, especially the Germanic elements of organ building techniques and traditions. As a result, hundreds of Allen Organs have already been installed in Japan, and I have every reason to believe that our success there will continue.

A most interesting situation recently occurred in Hong Kong. Some years ago we sold an organ to St. John's Anglican Cathedral in that city. Recently, the cathedral decided to upgrade their music program, and this required a more comprehensive instrument. One of our competitors attempted to capitalize on the situation. However, after considering our competitor's offering, the purchasing people of St. John's decided that even the old Allen was more satisfactory than our competitor's newest creation. Having passed this acid test, we were pleased to receive St. John's order for a new and much larger Allen to replace their smaller instrument.

One recent occurrence of particular interest concerns the new Basilique Notre Dame in Yamoussoukro, Ivory Coast, Africa. This building, according to an article in the *New York Times Magazine* on December 25, 1988, is the largest church building in the world next to St. Peter's in Rome. The construction of this edifice is scheduled for completion toward the end of 1989, at which time an Allen Digital Computer Organ will be installed.

Finally, while it may appear to the reader that I have assumed a complaining stance against many of the opposing factors that I have encountered in my fifty years as an organ builder, in actuality these factors represented mere bumps on the road. On the whole, my business experiences have been quite gratifying. Therefore, with few hindsight modifications, I would undoubtedly opt to do things essentially the same way if I had to do them all over again.